COLLIERS WAY

Cover: Batch of Old Mills Colliery.

Wheel from Kilmersdon Colliery in centre of Radstock

Colliers Way

History and Walks in the
Somerset Coalfield

Peter Collier

EX LIBRIS PRESS

First published in 1986
This new, revised edition
published in 1999 by
EX LIBRIS PRESS
1 The Shambles
Bradford on Avon
Wiltshire
BA15 1JS

Design and typesetting by
Ex Libris Press

Cover printed by
Shires Press
Trowbridge
Wiltshire

Printed and bound in Britain by
Cromwell Press
Trowbridge
Wiltshire

ISBN 0 948578 43 2

Contents

Bibliography

Niall Allsop: *The Somersetshire Coal Canal Rediscovered* (Millstream Books, 1988)

Robin Atthill: *Old Mendip* (David and Charles, 1964)

Robin Atthill: *The Somerset and Dorset Railway* (David and Charles, 1967)

Robin K Bluhm: *Bibliography of the Somerset Coalfield*

John Bulley: *To Mendip for Coal* (Proceedings of the Somerset Archaeology and Natural History Society, 1951-2)

Kenneth R Clew: *The Somersetshire Coal Canal and Railways* (David and Charles, 1970)

Kenneth R Clew: *The Dorset and Somerset Canal* (David and Charles, 1971)

C G Down and A J Warrington:*The History of the Somerset Coalfield* (David and Charles, 1971)

C G Down and A J Warrington: *The Newbury Railway* (Industrial Railway Society, 1979)

Fred Flower: *Somerset Coalmining Life* (Millstream Books, 1990)

Chris Handley: *Radstock Coal and Steam* (Millstream books, 1991)

Reg Jones: *Down Memory Lane* (1984)

C G Maggs: *The Bath to Weymouth Line* (Oakwood Press, 1982)

R J G Savage (editor): *Geological Excursions in the Bristol District* (University of Bristol, 1977)

John Skinner: *Journal of a Somerset Rector 1803-1834* (Oxford University Press, 1984)

David J Strawbridge: *Meandering Through Chilcompton* (David Strawbridge, 1985)

Mike Vincent: *Through Countryside and Coalfield* (Oxford Publishing Company, 1990)

David Warnock: *The Bristol and North Somerset Railway 1863-1884* (Temple Cloud Publications 1978)

D W Warnock and R G Parsons: *The Bristol and North Somerset Railway Since 1884* (Avon-Anglia Publications, 1979)

INTRODUCTION

I have travelled many times from Trowbridge, where I live, to Radstock and the surrounding small towns and villages. To the west of Faulkland, as I pass Turner's Terrace, I always feel that I am approaching a special part of England. At the crossroads I turn right and begin to descend Terry Hill. If it is a clear day I can always see the conical batch or waste tip of Old Mills Colliery beyond the houses of Midsomer Norton. This landmark is the most vivid reminder of the industrial past of North Somerset. It is this past which makes North Somerset a special place for me.

Further down Terry Hill are rows of cottages built for the miners, and other rows become visible on the north side of the valley, close to the landscaped batch of another colliery. In the 1950s Nikolaus Pevsner, in the North Somerset and Bristol volume of his 'The Buildings of England' series, said of Radstock that it was 'really desperately ugly' in the surrounding, pleasant countryside. Nowadays, most people think of this area as being all pleasant countryside. Yet locked away amongst the woods, fields and quiet villages is a complex, fascinating, industrial history.

It is difficult now to believe that along the valleys of this region there were dozens of coal mines, served by tramways, railways and canals. However, the signs are still there, despite much new building, and it is my intention in this book to try to unlock some parts of this history by directing you along paths and tracks to what remains. You will need to use your imagination, for many of the remains are little more than grass-covered mounds, so to help you I have included a brief history of the coalfield and its transport network and, very important, several interviews with miners who told me not only what it was like to work in the pits, but also what life was like in a mining community.

It is also worth referring to some of the new books about the area which have been published since the first edition of this book. Two in particular, *Radstock Coal and Steam* by Chris Handley and *Through Countryside and Coalfield* by Mike Vincent, include old photographs of the area and it is fascinating to compare these with the landscape today. My interest in the area stems from my childhood. I often travelled by train from Brislington station in Bristol to Frome and the journey was always interesting, especially the glimpse of the colliery incline at Pensford and the sight of the traffic held up in the centre of Radstock behind the double set of crossing gates. At other times I went on holiday to Bournemouth, travelling along the Somerset and Dorset line, with its long climb up out of Radstock past Norton Hill Colliery. I later discovered that my grandfather had been employed by Westbury Iron Works, and part of his job was to inspect the brickwork of the shafts of pits in the Mells area, presumably the Mells, Newbury and Mackintosh collieries. I then found in some of his old papers a plan of foundations for an Avery weighing machine. On the back is the date 25/5/14 and the instructions, 'For Enclosure to Llwydcoed Collieries Ltd., Coleford.'

When I moved to Trowbridge, thirty years ago, I began to walk some of the old railway lines in the area, especially the Somerset and Dorset, the Bristol to Frome line and the Hallatrow to Limpley Stoke branch. I soon came across the pamphlet by Down and Warrington on *The Newbury Railway* and, with some friends, I walked the route of this railway and discovered remains of the old Dorset and Somerset Canal, as well as the sites of Mackintosh and Newbury collieries.

Much later I found Down and Warrington's book on the Somerset coalfield and determined to find some of the other sites they described.

Apart from an interest in industrial archaeology, the most important factors which have inspired me to write this book have been, first, the pleasure I received from walking across the countryside of North Somerset, and second, the pleasure of talking to people associated with the coal industry. Once I had planned out the routes on the maps, I started to walk, and the more I walked the more I wanted to sample the pleasure of walking in this area. There was the fascination of discovering the grass-covered routes of old railways and the marshy beds of canals, and of finding, in quiet, almost wild, valleys, stark remains of buildings which were once part of a thriving coal mine. (Unfortunately, since the first edition, quite a few of the derelict buildings have disappeared.) Nearly every day that I set out walking I met at least one person who had worked in a mine or who, in some way, was connected with the mines. There still exists a great pride in these people. They remember their hard lives vividly and each one has some new insight to reveal.

Although no one would wish for those past times to return, or for people today to have to work in the same conditions, it is those very conditions which have made them proud of their achievements.

At about the time I was finishing writing the first edition of this book the first edition of *Five Arches* was published. This is the journal of the Radstock, Midsomer Norton and District Museum Society. It publishes fascinating articles about the area and often includes reminiscences of miners and the results of research into the history of the railways and canals. The society set up a museum in 1989 at Haydon and now (1999) the old market hall is being converted to house the exhibits. At Camerton a heritage trail has been set up with an information board about the colliery and it is to be hoped that other similar projects will be undertaken to ensure that this fascinating history is kept alive.

This book is two parts. Part One is concerned with the geological, historical and social background. There is a brief explanation of how the coalfield was formed and how the geology affected mining. Next there is a history of mining and the canals and railways which were developed to transport the coal. Finally in this section there are interviews with several ex-miners.

Part Two describes twelve walks. All are circular and most, if not all, can be walked easily in a morning or an afternoon. If you want an all-day walk it is often possible to walk two from the same starting point. For example, three of the walks start in the centre of Radstock, two begin at Coleford.

I have given a map reference for each starting point to help identify its position on the Ordnance Survey map. It is very useful to carry a map with you, especially the Pathfinder 1:25,000 maps

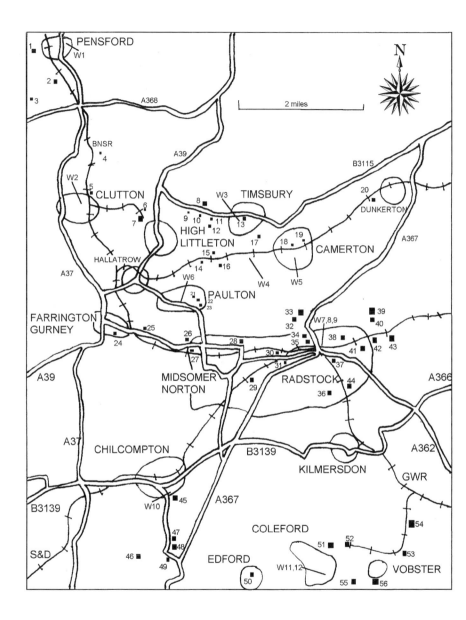

Opposite: Somerset Coalfield, showing roads, railways and collieries which are covered in the walks.

W1   Starting point of walks

Key to site of numbered mines:

1	Rydons	29	Norton Hill New
2	Pensford	30	Old Welton
3	Bromley	31	Wellsway
4	Frys Bottom	32	Clandown
5	Burchells	33	Smallcombe
6	Mooresland	34	Old Pit
7	Greyfield	35	Middle Pit
8	Hayeswood	36	Kilmersdon (Haydon)
9	Mearns	37	Ludlows
10	Amesbury	38	Tyning
11	New Tyning	39	Braysdown
12	Old Grove	40	Woodborough
13	Upper Conygre	41	Upper Writhlington
14	Paulton Engine	42	Lower Writhlington
15	Withy Mills	43	Foxcote
16	Radford	44	Huish
17	Lower Conygre	45	New Rock
18	Camerton Old	46	Moorewood New
19	Camerton New	47	Old Rock
20	Dunkerton	48	Strap
21	Paulton Ham	49	Sweetleaze
22	Paulton Hill	50	Edford
23	Simons Hill	51	Mackintosh
24	Marsh Lane	52	Newbury
25	Farrington	53	Bilboa
26	Old Mills	54	Mells
27	Springfield	55	Breach
28	Welton Hill	56	Vobster

which clearly show the routes of 'Dismantled Railway' and the sites of some of the collieries. (Also, I did make one or two mistakes in the first edition by writing 'right' instead of 'left'! I hope there are none in this edition.)

The Ordnance Survey has changed its maps since the first edition. You can still buy the Pathfinder maps, but the best buy is now the Explorer series. These are 2.5 inch maps which cover a much larger area. The two which will cover the whole of the area of the book, and a lot more beside, are: 155, Bristol and Bath (this covers Walk 1 and a small part of Walk 2); and 145, Shepton Mallet (this covers all the other walks).

Finally, what are the boundaries of the North Somerset Coalfield? Many books lump the Bristol coalfield with the North Somerset and most general books show them by one shaded area. However, the South Gloucestershire and Somerset basins are more or less separated from each other by what geologists call the Kingswood Anticline, and locally most people accept this division. At one time this area was, socially and culturally, a separate entity, bounded to the south by the Mendip Hills. There were mines in Nailsea, Bishop Sutton and Newton St. Loe, but because there is little to see in those areas I have planned walks in the following: in the north, Pensford on the River chew; in the centre, along the Cam Brook and Wellow Brook valleys; and in the south, the Nettlebridge Valley.

Abbreviations used in the descriptions of the walks are as follows:

BNSR	Bristol and North Somerset Railway
GWR	Great Western Railway
NCB	National Coal Board
S&D	Somerset and Dorset Railway
SCC	Somerset Coal Canal

The word 'batch' is used in North Somerset to refer to a dirt tip where the coal waste was deposited, but I do not know how long it has been used in this sense. The word 'batch' originally derived from the Old English word *bacan* which meant 'something baked'. In this sense it can mean loaves of bread. Perhaps Somerset people compared the shape of the waste tips to loaves of bread. Or is there another explanation?

GEOLOGY OF THE SOMERSET COALFIELD

For at least six centuries, many people's lives were bound up with the mining of coal in the North Somerset Coalfield. The coal was created millions of years ago and each coal seam took many centuries to form. A brief look at the geology of coal will explain why coal mining was so difficult in this area.

About 300 million years ago, what we now know as Britain was part of 'Euramerica', one of three large continents, which later, according to the theory of Plate Tectonics, moved slowly apart from each other across the surface of the Earth. This continent was situated in such a position that Radstock, had it then existed, would have been close to the equator and any inhabitant could have walked to North America without the inconvenience of crossing the Atlantic Ocean.

During this period of time, known as the Carboniferous Period, southern Britain was, at first, covered by a warm, shallow sea rather like the Caribbean of today. To the north lay an island stretching from what is now the east coast of Ireland, across the Midlands to East Anglia and into Belgium. It was at this time that the rocks that contain the coal seams were formed.

Gradually, the shallow sea near the island was turned into a swamp as rivers brought down mud and silt. Dense tropical forests grew in these swamps, but at times the sea would sweep over the newly formed land and the forests would be destroyed. The vegetation rotted and changed first to peat. Later, after being buried under thick layers of mud and sand, the peat changed into coal. This process would start again as the sea level changed and so another coal seam would be established. The term Coal Measures applies not just to the seams of coal, but to all those rocks, sandstones,

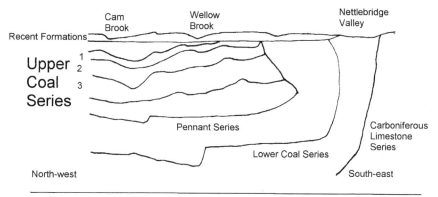

Cam Brook · Wellow Brook · Nettlebridge Valley

Recent Formations

Upper Coal Series
1
2
3

Pennant Series

Carboniferous Limestone Series

Lower Coal Series

North-west

South-east

1. Productive measures of Radstock Group 2. Barren Red Shales
3. Productive measures of Farrington Group

Generalised Section of the Coalfield

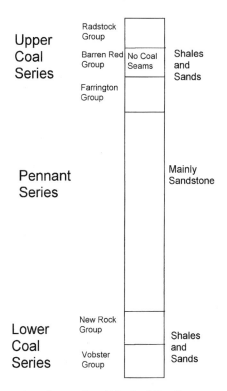

Upper Coal Series	Radstock Group		Shales and Sands
	Barren Red Group	No Coal Seams	
	Farrington Group		
Pennant Series			Mainly Sandstone
Lower Coal Series	New Rock Group		Shales and Sands
	Vobster Group		

Generalised Vertical Section

mudstones, shales, etc, which were laid down in these conditions.

After these coal measures were created about 180 million years ago, there occurred another series of events which made man's efforts at extracting the coal in North Somerset much more difficult. This is called the Hercynian Orogeny, named after mountain chains in Germany. Orogeny means mountain building and the terrific forces which formed mountain chains across Central Europe and Asia also sent shock waves across south-west England. The Mendips were raised up like a huge broken wave, part of a movement which stretched across to south-west Wales. The effect of these forces on the coal measures was to make them buckle and break up. Sometimes the coal seams became fantastically distorted, turning and twisting like a piece of ribbon; sometimes they snapped and one end of a seam was pushed along a fracture or fault. Alongside the Radstock Slide Fault the distance between the broken ends of a seam can be as much as 1,500 feet.

These disturbances meant that the coalfield was divided into several isolated basins, separated by ridges or hills from each other. In the west there is a group of small basins where coal has been found at Nailsea, Clapton and Avonmouth. In the north is the Parkfield-Coalpit Heath basin. To the south of this, separated by what is called the Kingswood Anticline, are the Pensford and Radstock basins. These two are themselves separated from each other by an area of great faulting often referred to as the Farmborough Fault or Farmborough Compression Zone. Coal has been mined in Bristol, especially in Bedminster and Kingswood as well as Bitton and there were mines at Newton St Loe, close to the Globe Inn and at Pennyquick Bottom at Twerton. In fact, in the nineteenth century a 'Report of the Commissioners appointed to enquire into the several matters relating to coal in the United Kingdom' listed over thirty parishes in North Somerset 'as being those in which coal had been worked at one time or another.' These included Chew Magna, Corston, Keynsham, Publow, Queen Charlton, Stanton Drew, Wellow and Wraxall with Failand.

The coal measures are often divided by geologists into three series depending on the time when they were laid down – the Upper Coal Series, the Pennant Series and the Lower Coal Series, the last being the oldest.

In the Lower coal Series are two groups of coal seams, the Vobster Group and the New Rock Group. The Vobster seams are named after the village where they come to the surface and it has been suggested that they were the first to be worked in Somerset. The coal is good coking coal, but unfortunately the seams are difficult and dangerous to work because of the distortion of the seams which are sometimes vertical. The New Rock Group is named after the New Rock Colliery. Of these two groups, twelve seams were extensively worked in the Newbury and Vobster district, although in the New Rock and Moorewood areas only eight seams could be worked as the others were too thin.

The Pennant Series consists of a very thick layer of sandstone which was laid down by a large river. The coal seams in this series have not been much worked in the Somerset Coalfield.

In the Upper Coal Series are two coal-bearing groups of rocks – the Radstock Group and the Farrington Group. These are separated by the Barren Red Group, layers of shales or clay rock, which do not contain any coal seams at all.

Pensford and Radstock mines worked mainly the Upper Coal Series, whereas the Nettlebridge Valley collieries worked mainly the Lower Coal Series.

The coal seams in the North Somerset Coalfield are not only often faulted, but they are also generally thin. For example, in the Farrington Group of seams only three of the five coals exceeded two feet in thickness. This means, of course, very difficult conditions for the miners. In 1873, John Anstie, who had worked on the Royal Commission mentioned above, published his own investigation, *The Coal Fields of Gloucestershire and Somersetshire*. He listed many of the collieries with details of the seams they were working. It is a fascinating historical document which reveals not only the thinness of the seams, but also the sometimes unusual local names give to them. At Old Mills Colliery he notes the following:

Cathead Seam (18 inches) at 200 yards
Farrington-Top Seam (18 inches) at 226 yards
Middle Seam (2 feet 4 inches) at 284 yards

Two-Coal Seam (18 inches) at 288 yards
Church-Close Seam (3 feet) at 342 yards.

He says of the seams: 'These are all good household coals, the 'Top' seam being the best.' Other names that are mentioned include 'Stinking', 'Peacock', 'Little' or 'Dabchick', 'Bull' and 'Hollybush'.

When coal mining ceased in the region, the coal seams remained geologically important for a time. Before the tips were covered by grass and trees, or reclaimed, fossils could still be found. In *Geological Excursions in the Bristol District* there is a chapter describing the best tips for collecting fossils. There were ferns and a few animal fossils to be found and at Tyning, near Radstock, a large dragonfly-like creature, *Boltonites radstockensis*, was collected.

HISTORY OF THE SOMERSET COALFIELD

The history of coal in North Somerset is a long one and I have divided it into two parts. The first period ends at the beginning of the nineteenth century. From this time on, as Down and Warrington note, 'Somerset mining began the long climb to the peak of its achievement, reached in the first decades of the twentieth century.' The concealed coalfield was then being exploited by deep mines and the inventions of the Industrial Revolution (especially the steam engine) were increasingly being used to make mining more efficient.

Up to 1800

Coal has been worked for centuries in North Somerset. Its use probably dates back to Roman times. In other parts of the country, along Hadrian's Wall, in lead smelting furnaces near Warrington and in remains in Manchester, coal and coal ash have been found. Caius Julius Solinus, a writer of the 3rd century AD, refers to a fuel used to make the sacred fire in the temple of Sulis Minerva at Bath. His description of undying fires has usually been interpreted as being a reference to coal. As coal outcrops were easily accessible close to the Roman road, the Fosseway, where it crosses the Nettlebridge valley, it is likely that the Romans had discovered and were using coal to a limited extent.

It is probable that coal was being dug up in the 13th century in and around North Somerset, though a mention to coal being used in Kilmersdon in 1305 could refer to charcoal. However, by the 15th century the raising of coal in the parish of Stratton-on-the-Fosse must have been a well-established industry. In 1460, for example, the 'coal-mine of the lord' of Stratton was leased to John Wolley or Welley who with his partners was paying a yearly rent of £1.6s.8d. By 1477, although the same firm was still at work, there were other people paying rent for the privilege of digging in the same area. In 1458 the wardens of St. John's, Glastonbury spent £4.3s.11d. on coal. And again, during the sixteenth and seventeenth centuries, there are many historical references to coal workings in this area. During the reign of Charles II it was reported that 'the forest of Mendipp where colepitts are or have been wrought doe extend in length between fowre and ffive miles and about one mile in breadth, and the mannours of Ashweeke, Kilmersdon, Holcombe, Mells, Babington, Luckington and Stratton are mannours bordering upon and adjoyneing to the forest of Mendipp.' Coal raised in these parishes was known as 'Mendip Coal' and it was common to talk of going to Mendip 'for coles'.

In Timsbury coal was being raised in the sixteenth century and probably had been for some time. In the seventeenth century there was a big increase in mining activity with important pits around Farrington Gurney and High Littleton, as well as in Clutton, Pensford, Midsomer Norton and Paulton amongst others. Open cast pits were being worked at Lower Vobster and coal was now being used in Bath and Wells.

Skilled labour for the mines was probably drawn from the lead mines of the Mendips – the word 'vein', used in lead mining, was used for a long time in Somerset rather than the more usual 'seam'. Other local words were 'dirt batch' for waste tip and 'gug' for a rope-worked incline.

It is difficult to estimate the amount of coal actually produced before 1800. Bulley, in his *To Mendip for Coal* suggests that near the end of the seventeenth century coal production might have reached 50,000 tons in a good year, but may not have reached 10,000 tons in a bad year.

In early times, coal was used mostly by smiths and lime-burners. Without proper chimneys coal smoke was too much of a nuisance for ordinary people to use, although coal must have been used extensively in London as there was a Royal Proclamation as early as 1316 against the use of coal because of the pollution it caused. The shortage of wood in Tudor times, though, meant that coal was used more and more as a domestic fuel – and chimneys began to be added to houses.

Originally, coal workings were established where coal outcrops at the surface. It was dug out from shallow excavations and later from simple pits called bell pits. A shaft of between three to five feet in diameter was sunk and then the coal all around the shaft was dug out. The shafts were often widened or 'belled' out until they became dangerous, and then a new shaft would be started to reach the seam of coal further along. Dirt from the new shaft was used to fill up the old one. The method of surveying was often as follows: 'Forepitch is sometimes made, which is by sinking pits, ten, twenty, thirty or forty yards before the place the coal outed and near on the same point of the compass either east or west.' Dowsing was also used, and it appears that the whole method was a little hit or miss.

Such pits could not go very deep because of drainage and ventilation problems, but by the 15th century there were underground workings in Somerset, and in 1437 at Kilmersdon there was one pit with a drainage channel. As ways of draining the pits and winding up men and coal were found, so the pits got deeper. In 1610 a surveyor reported on one of the pits in Clutton (one fathom equals six feet):

'There be now three pits near widow blackers house the highest about 4 fathoms, the middle six fathoms, the lowest 8 fathoms deep. At these depths they cut out their lanes about 4 feet high and broad. They need no great store of timber work for support. The lane we crept through was a good quoits length, wherein we found but two cross lanes, whereby it may appear that the mine is but newly entered into. They now work in two pits at once, and have below two or three men and four or five boys, and also three men to wind up the coals. At the end of every lane a man worketh, and there maketh his bench, as they call it, and according to the vent they make more or fewer benches. The wages allowed to the men is to him that has most 4s. the week, and to the boys 1s.6d. Adding for candles, increase of wages for work by night, ropes, sharpening of tools, baskets, etc., the whole week's charge may arise to £3. Reckoning 100 horse loads a day at 3d. the receipt coming to £7 10s. the week, and the net gain is £4.10s. of which one-fourth for the tenant, and the rest remaineth for the lord. It is said that the works at Timsbury are near worn out, and all smiths use the coal of Clutton and none of Timsbury.'

The method of working coal described here is called 'pillar and stall' and at this time was the usual way in English coal mines. Large pillars of coal were left untouched to support the roof and, although such a method needed no expensive wooden supports, a great deal of coal was left behind.

After the Restoration in 1660 there are many notices of coal mining in Somerset, several referring to explosions of firedamp. For example, during the reign of Charles II this report occurs:

'... about 2 miles on the south-east of Stony Easton at a place bordering to Mendip Hills begins a running of coal consisting of several veins which extends itself towards the East about 4 miles. There is much working in this running and firedamps continually there happen, so that many men of late years have been killed, many others maimed and a multitude burnt.'

By 1719, gunpowder was being used to break through the hard beds of rock, although in the Mendip lead-mines it had been used as early as 1683. This is the first recorded use of gunpowder in a British coal mine.

By 1725 the 'pillar and stall' way of working had been superseded in Somerset by the long wall system which meant that, although more timber was needed, nearly all the coal could be extracted, and much of the rubbish could be pushed back in the space left. There was one coalface, no more that 30 yards wide, with two or three hewers working there. Carting boys took the coal in 'putts' to the main roadway. A putt was a kind of sledge with a container for coal on top made out of hazel rods wrapped round iron pins, and was very heavy even before several hundredweights of coal were put in it. The boys (often men!) used the famous or infamous 'guss and crook' to haul these putts over the rough ground with only a candle to light their way. The guss was made usually of rope and fitted tightly round the waist. To it was attached an iron chain and a hook, the crook, about eight inches long and made from a half inch iron bar. The chain and hook hung down at the front, passed through the legs and the hook was attached to the putt. The carting boy then pulled the putt forward, usually horizontal to the floor, often on hands and knees. You can imagine the effect this rope would have on the bare skin of the boy. They might also have been working in bare feet so that they could gain a good foothold on the rough ground.

This sounds a primitive method of haulage and yet it lasted well into the twentieth century. I have spoken to miners who worked in this way for years, barefoot and sometimes naked, with the wax from the candle in their helmet dripping on to their faces and bodies.

At the main road the coal was transferred to a larger type of putt called a 'wreath-cart', again made partly from hazel rods which would then be attached to the pit rope, and hauled to the shaft. Here the coal was transferred to wicker baskets which were then wound up the shaft. At first the shafts in Somerset were very narrow, usually only four feet in diameter, though by 1800 some had increased to five feet. They were usually circular.

One of the most common ways for the men and boys to ascend and descend the pit was by the 'hooker'. A loop of rope which went round a man's thigh was attached by a hook to the chain at the end of the pit rope. The miner would then hang on to the pit rope and, with perhaps ten other miners, would descend like, Bulley aptly notes, a string of onions. Sometimes a boy would sit on the miner's lap!

The general method for winding coal was the horse drum. This was a horizontal drum fixed over the shaft, around which was wound the rope, and turned by horses. A later and popular improvement placed the drum away from the shaft. The ropes from it went over pulleys at the top of the shaft before going down the shaft itself. Later on water wheels were sometimes used.

In the region round Vobster the seams of coal were often vertical and a different method of mining had to be adopted, one similar to 'stoping' in lead mines. With this method the miners would work up the seam. They would work out the coal above their heads, then put down timbers to stand on, so that they could move higher up the seam and so on.

Ventilation of the pits was another problem which had to be dealt with. One miner told me that when he started working, at the beginning of the 20th century, there was so little air at the coalface that his candle would hardly burn. In order that his father, with whom he was working, could get enough oxygen to work properly he had to wave his shovel backwards and forwards to create a draught! The most common method, used into the 20th century, was that of a furnace which was lit at the bottom of one of the two shafts causing air to circulate round the working. One writer, in 1700, describes an iron basket being lowered down the shaft filled with burning coal 'to draw the stenched or stagnant air from the bottom and the lanes.' Firedamp was not a problem except around Coleford, Vobster and Mells, where over the centuries there were many gas explosions and fatalities.

As the mines became deeper so there were increasing problems with getting rid of the water that accumulated. At first, ditches or drainage channels were dug, and then adits were excavated through the hillside into a nearby river or stream. But as the mines went deeper than the valley bottom new methods had to be employed. Pumps, driven by water wheels, were in use as early as 1610, and others used manpower, or horsepower. Such pumps lasted into the nineteenth century in many pits, but it was this never-ending problem of getting rid of water which produced what R.A.Buchanan has called 'the first and greatest contribution of the steam engine to the coal industry.'

In 1698 Thomas Savery patented his steam engine which he nicknamed 'The Miner's Friend' because of its application in pumping water out of mines. A more reliable engine came in 1712 when Thomas Newcomen made his first steam beam pumping engine. Although there might have been such an engine in use at Paulton in 1750 it was not until after about 1780 that such engines, or those developed by Boulton and Watt, came to be used more generally in Somerset. It is interesting to compare this with the situation in the Tyneside coalfield where it has been calculated there were at least a hundred 'fire-engines' of the Newcomen type at work by 1756.

It is this kind of contrast that highlights another difference between the Somerset Coalfield and others in Britain. When steam power and mechanisation came, Somerset was unable to keep up. As virtually no other important industries developed alongside the coal mines in Somerset, as they did elsewhere, capital for improvements had to come from the local mine owners. In other regions, for example South Wales, the 'Black Country', South Yorkshire and Teesside, important iron industries were set up. In Somerset, the only important foundry in the coalfield was Paulton Foundry, established by 1810.

Bulley distinguishes three main groups of mine owners in the period up to 1830. The first, important up to the mid-eighteenth century, consisted of colliers themselves who leased small mines. After the mid-seventeenth century, men with money to invest took an interest in speculating in mining, although few took an active part in the actual process of running the business. The third and most important group consisted of wealthy landowners who either mined coal on their own land or invested in mines on other people's land. The important point to remember is that the owners were local and money to invest in the mines had to come from local sources.

One of these local landowning families, the Waldegraves, in 1749 allowed James Lansdown, in partnership with others, to take a 42 year lease to explore for coal on its estate in Radstock. In 1763, after 14 years – 14 years! – coal was found and Old Pit started work. It is not certain on what grounds coal was thought to be here. J. Anstie, in his fascinating *Coalfields of Gloucestershire and Somerset*, published in 1873, comments rather wryly:

'Discovery of coal at Radstock must be regarded more as an accident than anything else ... it is not probable that those who sunk the Old Pit at Radstock had any clear notion of the geological structure of the Upper Series basin at that date.'

This discovery was certainly the most important event in the coalfield in the eighteenth century, and probably the most significant event in the history of the North Somerset Coalfield. The concealed coalfield had been opened up and the Radstock district now led the way, with new pits being opened and new techniques being adopted.

The eighteenth century saw other changes which encouraged the expansion of the coalfield. There was a rising demand for coal, much of which was used in the limekilns. Lime was necessary in the production of mortar for building purposes and, with the agricultural improvements being made in this century, it was in great demand as manure by farmers. Coke was also in demand for use in breweries to dry malt, and at High Littleton and at Writhlington coke was being produced specifically for this purpose. The greater part, though, was for the domestic market and until the Somerset Coal Canal was opened in the 19th century most went to local markets within a few miles radius. To the south-west was Glastonbury and the villages and farms on the Mendips. Further west, though, villages along the coast were being supplied with coal brought in by sea, mainly from South Wales. Bristol, in the north, had its own local coalfield and little coal from Somerset was sold there. But Bath was an important market and coal was also delivered to west Wiltshire and to Shepton Mallet in the south.

Transport was an age-old problem. Moving coal from the collieries to the customers, across the hills and valleys of north Somerset, was not a straightforward business. Anyone who has walked or cycled northwards or southwards in the area will know what the problems are. In the north-east of England, Tyneside was exporting coal to the heart of London from the sixteenth century onwards – by sea. There were no convenient ports in north Somerset, no navigable rivers, and the only ways of carrying coal were on a man's back in a sack, in panniers on horses, or in wagons. The largest wagon could carry no more than about three tons and the roads were in a very poor state until the Turnpike Trusts started their work in the 18th century. In fact, the mode and speed of transport had hardly changed since Roman times.

Roads had got worse during the Middle Ages, not better, and coal wagons were often responsible for making them even worse during the sixteenth and seventeenth centuries. In 1617 there was a complaint from the villagers of Stoke St Michael, between Coleford and Shepton Mallet, that 'of late by reason of many coal mines which are set to work in the country near there adjoining, there is so much travelling that way that the highways there are much in decay and grown very founderous', that is, muddy! Things got so bad that in 1654 an Act was passed which restricted the number of animals used to haul one coal wagon. John Wesley, when he passed through Somerset, commented that Midsomer Norton must be so called because it was impossible to reach it at any other time of year.

However, the Turnpike Trusts began, slowly, to change all this. The people of a parish no longer had to maintain the main roads that went through their district. A system of tolls, collected and spent by the Trusts, meant effectively that road users paid for the upkeep. A network of roads was established, the first locally being that of Bath in 1707. Others followed, Bristol in 1727, Frome in 1757 and Buckland Dinham (later Radstock) in 1768. By the end of the century there was good road access to the surrounding towns, but it had taken a long time.

Not surprisingly, the miners resented the tolls they had to pay, despite the fact that their coal could be transported more easily and further afield, and they even seem to have attacked the toll houses. However, John Billingsley, a famous Somerset man, owner of Oakhill Brewery, involved in all the local canal companies and an agricultural expert, as well as a member of various Turnpike Trusts, wrote at the end of the 18th century:

> 'Before the turnpike roads were established, coal was carried on horses' backs to the distance of fifteen or twenty miles from the collieries; each horse carried about two hundred and a half weight. Now one horse, with a light cart, will draw ten hundred weight, or four times than a horse could carry. Can an insignificant toll be put in competition with this saving?'

Nevertheless, although the colliery owners eventually accepted the necessity of good roads, and even in some cases made payments to keep roads in good repair, the tolls did lead to higher coal prices. Also, the better roads meant that coal from other fields, especially the Welsh, could be brought in more easily than before. This was always one of the paradoxes of this coalfield – that, as transport improved, especially the coming of canals and railways, allowing easier export of coal from the region, so 'foreign' coal from Wales and the North was more easily imported.

The Industrial Age

At the beginning of the nineteenth century there were about 4,000 people employed in the coalfield. Villages such as Farrington Gurney, High Littleton, Radstock, Camerton, Paulton and Midsomer Norton were growing in size, partly because of the developing industry. Two canals had been proposed in the 1790's and were being constructed, steam winding was introduced at Middle Pit in Radstock in 1804, more than doubling the daily output to 50 tons, and William Smith's studies of the strata of the local mines were beginning to help the mine owners understand the nature of the seams they were working.

The canals and railways I shall deal with in more detail in the next chapter, but it is necessary to give a brief outline here of their rise and fall to show how they affected and were affected by the coalfield.

The two canals were the Somerset Coal Canal, from the Kennet and Avon Canal to Paulton and to Radstock, and a branch of the Dorset and Somerset Canal from Frome to the Nettlebridge Valley. Both were difficult to construct, partly because of engineering difficulties, but mainly because of financial problems. A national financial crisis in 1793 and the outbreak of war with France took many people's minds off canal building, although the actions of French privateers off the south-west coast of England made others keen to link the English and Bristol Channels to avoid sailing round the hazardous Cornish coast. This was an important consideration to those planning the Dorset and Somerset Canal. They wished to connect Bristol to the Dorset coast at Poole, via the River Avon, the proposed Kennet and Avon Canal and the new canal. The branch from Frome to Coleford and Edford it was hoped would provide much valuable coal traffic.

Lack of money finally defeated the Dorset and Somerset Canal, but the Somerset Coal Canal was constructed and its northern branch was very successful for a time. The southern branch was more difficult to work and eventually it was transformed into a tramroad.

This new method of transport helped the collieries around Radsock and Paulton to develop rapidly (though old collieries at Queen Charlton and Pensford soon closed). Coal could now be sent widely across southern Britain as far east as Reading along the Kennet and Avon and the Wilts and Berks Canals, both of which opened in 1810. Important customers were the mills of the local woollen industry which were changing over to steam power. Both Bradford-on-Avon and Trowbridge were alongside the Kennet and Avon Canal, and Somerset coal was cheaper for their mills than it was for many mills in the West Riding of Yorkshire. Trowbridge had steam plant as early as 1805, and between 1815 and 1835 steam power was adopted everywhere to drive the new machinery.

Coal also was used to manufacture gas and in the 1820's Bath had its first gas lighting installed. Midsomer Norton followed suit in 1840, providing another important outlet for Somerset coal. The population was increasing: between 1801 and 1831, Bath's population increased from 27,000 to 38,000, Frome's from 8,000 to 12,000. This meant a big increase in demand for coal to burn in new homes.

When the railways arrived other outlets were formed. The first line reached the coalfield in 1854. The Wilts, Somerset and Weymouth Railway Company had reached Frome by the time it was taken over by the Great Western Railway in 1850. A broad gauge branch to Radstock was built, at first for coal traffic, and this meant coal could be transported quickly and efficiently to Bath and other places on the GWR. By about 1858 there was also a branch from Mells Road to the collieries of Vobster, Mells and Coleford. This halted their decline for a while, much of this coal going to Westbury Iron Works. It was not until 1873, however, that the Bristol and North Somerset Railway opened its line from Bristol to Radstock. This was a standard gauge line, and in 1874 the Radstock to Frome section was converted, allowing through running from Bristol to Frome without a break of gauge. Also in 1874, the Somerset and Dorset Railway opened its line from Evercreech to Bath to join up with the Midland Railway which had reached Bath in 1869.

Customers included the iron works at Mells and Paulton, Whiteways the cider-makers at Whimple, breweries in the Midlands and firms in Newbury and Martock. The presence of the coalfield also influenced the setting up of new industries. For example, in 1848, a Mr Moulton returned from America and started processing rubber in a disused woollen mill in Bradford-on-Aon, where he could easily buy coal transported along the Somerset Coal and Kennet and Avon Canals.

The collieries slowly adapted to new ideas and techniques. Steam power gradually spread to all the main collieries for both pumping and winding, so that mines were able to be made deeper and more productive. In 1817, Clandown shaft was 1,200 feet deep, the deepest in the coalfield at that time. (The deepest ever was at Strap Colliery near Downside, 1,838 feet in the 1870's). The old wreath carts were replaced by iron 'hudges' after 1800. These were a kind of iron barrel, some of which were eventually big enough to hold up to a ton of coal. By the mid-nineteenth century, tubs with wheels were running on rails underground, often drawn by pit ponies. Before about 1850, flat hemp ropes were used in the shafts, then in mid-century wire ropes were introduced with cages and guides. The narrow shafts had to be widened to cope with them. As well as pumping engines, another common method of drainage was to use tanks in or under the cages to bring up water from the sump of the shaft.

Children of six or seven years old were employed at the pits at this time. There were several being employed at the Vobster collieries, for example. They opened and shut ventilation doors, pushed along the carriages of coal or helped in other simple tasks.

In the middle of the century, Frances, Dowager Countess of Waldegrave, a remarkable woman, daughter of a famous singer, and skilful at marrying the right men, directed that the pits of her Radstock coalworks be improved. Her manager from 1863 was James McMurtie, who stayed until his retirement in 1904. He wrote and spoke a great deal about the coalfield, giving a clear view of how the mines were worked. Shafts were widened to take two cages and guides, new machinery was installed and steam power increased. Other mines that could afford to do so followed suit. Compared with companies in other coalfields, though, these local businesses were still relatively small concerns.

In 1884, McMurtie took a large party from the Somerset Archaeology and Natural History Society down Ludlows Pit. The account of the trip and his talk to the group beforehand makes interesting reading:

'Having reached the coal by driving through the rock from the bottom of the shafts, they opened out the mineral, working it out continuously without any pillars to support the roof... The roads were laid with train rails, and the coal was brought from the face to the bottom of the shaft in trains worked by horse or engine power. They worked in that district the thinnest seams that were to be met with in any part of England, and when visitors inspected the mine, they would see what trouble and expenses were incurred to obtain the coal and probably they would not grumble so much at their coal bills. Some of the seams in Stafordshire were very thick, but in Radstock they worked veins only 14 inches in thickness. There was a certain quantity of debris produced from the shales which over- and under-laid the coal: it was not only sufficient to fill up the spaces caused by the extraction of the coal, but they had to raise large quantities to the surface. The roads underground were made six feet high, and to a certain extent they were timbered up.'

When the group arrived at the bottom of the shaft, they found 'the roadways brilliantly illuminated by some thousands of candles... During a walk of about a mile, the face of the coal was inspected and men seen at their work. Several fossil plants were pointed out in situ. Mr McMurtie accompanied the party, doing all in his power to make the ramble pleasant and profitable. The courtesy of the men, too, was most marked.'

Because most of the seams were thin it was relatively expensive to excavate large enough roads to take the large tubs. Because of this the guss and crook was still in use up to the 1930's in Somerset and even up to 1949 at Marsh Lane Pit.

Between 1870 and 1879, output from the coalfield reached 650,000 tons a year, more than double what it was in 1800, and the towns and villages continued to grow. This was not the same pattern everywhere in Britain. Although the population of most small towns and villages steadily increased in the first part of the 19th century, there was a big decline after the middle of the century because of the collapse of the woollen industry, the importation of American cereals and, with the expanding railway system, a consequent growth of the larger towns and cities. Midsomer Norton, Radstock and Paulton, however, continued to increase in size. In 1801 their combined population was 3,080; in 1851 it was 7,695; in 1901 it was 11,527.

The 1875 edition of Kelly's Post Office Directory of Somersetshire has this to say of Radstock:

> 'Since the formation of these lines of rail, the coal and passenger traffic has been greatly augmented, and the place is becoming a town; numerous dwellings have been erected; 50 villas, shops and other buildings are now in course of construction, and the whole of the central part of the parish has been lotted for building purposes. A local Board has been formed; likewise a School Board. A flourishing Working Men's Institute was established here in 1866, lotted the site for which, together with £300, was given by the Countess Waldegrave.'

In 1882 a railway was built from Hallatrow to Camerton to link up with the collieries in the Cam Valley, and this meant the end for the Somerset coal Canal. It finally closed in 1894 and the GWR bought it so that its branch could be extended to Limpley Stoke. Despite the coming of the railways, only about one third of the coal was actually transported by rail, the rest going by road as it had always done.

At the beginning of the 20th century another change was apparent. The old, smaller pits had mainly closed and the central area around Radstock was flourishing. Production reached its highest level – 1,3000,000 tons in 1901. Although there were now 10 mines in the Radstock area and 11 around Paulton, the mines in the south were still important, especially as they had their own Newbury railway. Some old pits were developed and new ones opened, notably those at Pensford, Dunkerton and Norton HIll.

The boom lasted only a few years. In the 1920's and 1930's many pits closed down and by the mid-thirties only fourteen were left.

In 1947 when the mines were nationalised there were still twelve working, but their owners had been slow to modernise them and they all suffered from lack of proper maintenance as well as a shortage of labour. Norton Hill and Pensford were comparatively new, but all the others were between 70 and 150 years old. At first the National Coal Board tried hard, and the more lucrative pits were modernised with screening plants, electric winding engines, coal ploughs and trunk conveyors. Money was mainly spent on Norton Hill, Old Mills, New Rock, Writhlington and Kilmersdon collieries, so that by 1959 these were the only ones left.

The 1960's brought new fuels to challenge coal – gas from North Africa and the North Sea, oil and nuclear power. The only large market left was Portishead Power Station, and even then the coal had to be mixed with midlands coal because it was so dirty.

Norton Hill and Old Mills closed in 1966. In September 1969 New Rock closed. In the year 1966-7 it had made a profit of about £10,000, and produced about 350 tons daily, but major faulting in the seam meant that it had to close. In 1972 came more bad news: Portishead ceased taking coal from Somerset as it was converted to oil burning. Coal was still being sent to Usk Power Station, but Writhlington and Kilmersdon pits were losing money at the rate of about £1,000 a day, or £250,000 a year on an annual production of about 125,000 tons. There was an attempt to open up a new 150 yard seam at Kilmersdon, but it was found to be badly faulted. In May 1973 came the news that both Kilmersdon and Writhlington were to close in September. There was little opposition to the closure, the miners accepting the inevitable. For over a year a few men continued to work dismantling the colliery for salvage and filling in pit shafts - four at Camerton, two at Radstock, two at Kilmersdon and two at Writhlington – using spoil from Kilmersdon tip.

Later, shale was extracted from Kilmersdon pit, an operation which caused local antagonism because of noise and dirt.

Periodically there were requests from mineral operators wishing to reclaim coal and shale from other pits in the area, including Pensford, Dunkerton, Old Mills and Tyning, and local residents were angry when eventually in 1983 a local firm was allowed to rework Writhlington tip after months of debate. The plan was to excavate the spoil heap and process it by washing it on site. After separation of the coal, discarded material would be re-tipped on the site, resulting in a tip similar to the original one though lower in size. It was calculated that the working was capable of producing 10 per cent coal, 350 tonnes a week, and 15 per cent burnt shale, 500 tonnes a week. It was also estimated that it could take up to six years to take out around 75,000 tonnes of shale and coal for sale to power stations and the construction industry. This work has now finished and the batch has been planted with trees.

During the 1984 miners' strike, pickets arrived in Radstock. They had come from the Six Bells Colliery in Abertillery, because small coal from Writhlington was being sent to the cement works in Westbury, Wiltshire. They stayed a week enjoying the peaceful picketing outside the site of the old colliery, and camped out at the Somerset Miners' Association building in Radstock.

For over 600 years there were coal miners in Somerset working in one of the most hazardous occupations ever devised, and building up a tradition of which the local community is justifiably proud. Yet the story is often one of conflict, death and difficulties for the miners themselves. Reading the local newspapers gives some idea of how tough life must often have been. For example, 1791, eleven die in a fire at the pit at Mells; 1796, a miner dies in a 'pond of boiling water' at Timsbury; 1852, two twelve-year-old boys die, one at Braysdown, the other at Hayeswood; 1929, an inquest into the death of a miner from silicosis; 1931, JS Haldane's publication, 'Silicosis and coal mining' draws attention to the pioneering work of F. Swift, Somerset miners' agent, in bringing the disease into public notice; 1931, another inquest into death from silicosis, the nineteenth since the war; 1932, death of a miner at 90, who had worked in the mines from the age of eight to seventy-three. There are numerous reports of strikes – 1792, 2,000 miners on strike for a week; 1872, 400 miners strike at Timsbury. In 1874 the Somersetshire award means that wages are first reduced by twenty-three-and-a-half percent. A strike follows and in 1875 the wages are reduced by eleven per cent. In 1876 a further seventeen per cent reduction is threatened. And in 1929 the Report of the Departmental Committee on the use of the guss in Somerset mines finds that it is 'not demonstrably harmful to the health of the wearer (but) was felt to be a relic of older and worse times.'

Is it surprising that there are reports of rioting and other disturbances? In 1796 colliers riot in Frome, also in 1813. In 1817 there are riots in Radstock and Paulton and in 1847 there are 'disturbances' in Radstock over food prices. In 1872 Clandown miners meet to form a union

But it is not all doom and gloom. In 1876 Lady Waldegrave graciously pays for a Radstock colliers' trip to Weymouth. And in 1931 pithead baths are installed at Pensford, the first in Somerset. In 1941, the collieries close for a one week paid holiday, the first holiday with pay for the miners. Then in 1944, there is a report on a case of pneumoconiosis.

In 1867, Seward W. Brice wrote, in *The Coal-field of North Somersetshire* (printed incidentally in Coleford):

'It seems scarcely credible that a Coal-field, the centre of which is barely in a straight line one hundred miles from the metropolis, should be raising so little coal annually that it will take more than three thousand years to exhaust it!'

Little more than a hundred years after these words were written, all the mines had closed. Brice could not have foreseen the tremendous social and technological changes that would take place in those hundred years, one of which would be the decline in the use of coal.

CANALS AND RAILWAYS

Although canal and rail transport were important to the coal industry in North Somerset, for various reasons the bulk of the coal went by road to the customer and, as we have seen, for most of its history the coalfield supplied coal mainly to a local, domestic market. Nevertheless, the coal canal was successful and well-used up until the time the railways took over its function. The railways, which were built originally to tap the coal traffic, might have hoped to survive on passenger and other freight traffic once the coal traffic disappeared, but the bus and particularly the car were more convenient for people, and passenger trains had disappeared on the Bristol-Frome line for several years before Beeching was able to act.

There are still many signs of the railways to be seen, the trackbed, bridges, stations, cuttings and embankments, and I have tried to point out many of these in the walks. Surprisingly, there are still signs of the canals, bridges and, in a few places, the bed of the canals. You can even find the old locks in places, although the best examples, around Coombe Hay, are not seen in the walks I have described. Even fragments of the unfinished Dorset and Somerset Canal are visible, and two of the walks follow its towpath for a short distance.

Dorset and Somerset Canal

The Somerset Coal Canal and the Dorset and Somerset Canal were proposed to tap the coal of the North Somerset Coalfield, and both were conceived at about the same time in 1792, although the latter can hardly be said to have started life.

The 1790's were difficult times for canal builders. Speculation had become a mania in the 18th century, but in 1792 there was the inevitable crash as war with France seemed likely. It is not surprising, therefore, that the Dorset and Somerset Canal was never finished. It is surprising, perhaps, that it ever got started, for the plan was a grand one, to link Poole on the English Channel to Bristol and the Bristol Channel. The main products to be carried would be coal, going south, and potter's clay going north from Wareham to the Potteries. The original plan was to start from Poole Harbour and continue through Wareham, Puddletown, Sturminster Newton, Wincanton and Frome to Bath, joining the newly proposed Kennet and Avon Canal near Freshford. A branch was projected from Frome along the Nettlebridge Valley to the Mendip collieries.

The engineer was Robert Whitworth, also consulting engineer to the Thames and Severn canal, but as he was very busy he recommended that his assistant take over the job. William Bennett also seems to have been busy as his report was not ready until 1795. A different route was settled on at the northern end, so that the canal would go via Beckington and Rode from Frome to join the Kennet and Avon Canal at Widbrook, close to the road from Trowbridge to Bradford-on-Avon. At the southern end there seems to have been difficulty in obtaining land, so that when the Dorset and Somerset Canal Bill was approved by parliament in 1796, it was intended to go only as far south as Gains Cross, south-east of Sturminster Newton. Presumably it was thought that the coal could be distributed by road from this point. The main part of the route was 49 miles long and the branch 11 miles.

The Act had stipulated that the branch should be built first and work had started by September 1796 at Edford.

Bennett, meanwhile, had also been appointed as an engineer to the Somerset Coal Canal, which had received its Royal Assent in 1794. Presumably, because a new type of caisson lock to Robert Weldon's design was being tried out on this canal at Coombe Hay, Bennett decided that a similar type of lock should be installed on the Dorset and Somerset. (Caisson means a watertight chamber). The first public trial was in 1798, but it was not at first successful. The same year James Fussell patented his design for a caisson lock. He was an edge tool maker, and a member of a famous local family, well-known for its ironworks near Mells during the eighteenth and nineteenth centuries. He was also one of the leading directors of the canal, and it may have been this fact which made Bennett suggest its use for the canal.

Fussell's canal lift involved the use of two counter-balancing caissons. Each watertight caisson was an open wooden box, big enough for a barge to float into. When hatches had been closed to seal off the lock, one caisson would descend to the lower level and the other would rise up. The caissons were moved by the use of chains and the difference in level at Barrow Hill, near Mells, where the lift was successfully tried out in 1800, was twenty feet. The committee was suitably impressed, and let contracts for five similar locks.

Unfortunately, the other locks were never finished. By 1803, the money raised for the building of the canal had been spent. England was expecting a French invasion at any time, and few people were interested in spending more money on the project. About nine miles had been cut when the canal was abandoned, but work never started on the main part of the canal.

Somerset Coal Canal

The Somerset Coal Canal was not a grand cross-country scheme like the Dorset and Somerset, but a small canal which met the needs of a group of colliery owners who worried that coal from other fields, especially from South Wales, would soon be available more cheaply than their own coal in local markets.

In December 1792, a meeting was held at the Old Down Inn, near Chilcompton, to plan a canal to Bath. After another meeting the following February, John Rennie was appointed to make a survey of the route. Rennie was in the area working on the Western Canal, later called the Kennet and Avon Canal, and was soon to become one of the most famous engineers in the country. When he died in 1821 he was buried in St. Paul's Cathedral. He was responsible for such projects as the Waterloo, Southwark and the new London bridges over the Thames, the London Docks, the East and West India docks, as well as bridges, canals and the breakwater at Plymouth. Much of the surveying of the Somerset Coal Canal route, though, was carried out by one of Rennie's assistants, William Smith, who also became famous, as the 'father of English geology'. (There is more about Smith in Walk 3).

The canal was to join the Kennet and Avon at Limpley Stoke. It was thought that a link here, almost in Wiltshire rather than nearer to Bath, would mean that Somerset coal would corner the market in Wiltshire, and South Wales coal would be unable to compete successfully. From Limpley Stoke the canal would follow Midford Brook to Midford, where it would divide into two arms, one following Cam Brook to Paulton, and the other following Wellow Brook to Radstock. Tramroads would transport coal from the collieries to wharves along the canal.

A draft bill was approved in February 1794, and it received the Royal Assent in April, the same year as the Kenet and Avon.

The two routes did not follow the two brooks exactly. On the northern branch locks were proposed at Combe Hay, and along the southern branch there was a steep gradient between Twinhoe and Midford. Whatever the reasons for incorporating these steep rises in level, they were to cause many difficulties, both technical and financial.

At Combe Hay it was decided to experiment with Robert Weldon's caisson lock in an attempt to save money, but the problems associated with its installation caused money to be wasted instead. Unlike Fussell's lock on the Dorset and Somerset Canal near Mells, there was only one caisson, also made of wood, eighty feet long, ten-and-a-half feet wide and eleven-and-a-half feet deep. This was raised and lowered in a stone chamber and, although there were initially some problems with the mechanism, it was eventually the fact that the stone chamber began to bulge that caused the abandonment of the scheme. It was discovered a few years ago that the stone chamber was excavated in Lower Fuller's Earth Clay which can absorb water and expand. It was this property of the clay soil that must have caused the failure of the lock. In a different situation it might very well have worked successfully. Trials started at the beginning of 1798. In 1799 the Prince of Wales watched a successful demonstration, but in 1800 it was decided to build an inclined plane to carry barges from one level to another.

Meanwhile, part of the canal was in operation. In mid-1798 it was reported that at least two-thirds of the canal was completed, and in October there was traffic on it between Camerton and Dunkerton.

In 1799, William Smith was sacked! It was said that he had mixed his own affairs with those of the canal company by buying a cottage near to the canal excavations at Tucking Mill near Midford. Quite what this meant is not known. Another suggestion is that he left, or was sacked, because of his underestimating of the costs of the canal.

The northern branch was completed by 1801. The inclined plane was now operating, and coal could be taken on to the Kennet and Avon Canal, which was partially open, and also on to the Wilts and Berks Canal. This canal, which joined the Kennet and Avon at Semington, near Melksham, was by this time open as far as Wootton Bassett.

It was not long before the decision was made to replace the inclined plane at Combe Hay with conventional locks. This involved curving the canal around the side of the hill and down the valley. Nineteen new locks had to be constructed, along with a Boulton and Watt engine to pump water back to the top of the locks. The locks were ready in 1805; the engine began work the following year.

Along the southern branch to Radstock there were more serious problems. It seems that so much money had been spent on the branch to Paulton that there was not enough left to make this branch a success. Instead of installing locks between Midford and Twinhoe, a mile-long railway was built so that coal had to be transhipped from canal to railway and back to canal again. Originally the canal was going to be built as far as Welton, but now it finished in the centre of Radstock, with the basin just to the south of the Waldegrave Arms Hotel. Tramroads connected with the collieries at Clandown and Welton. By 1812 this canal was hardly used and a few years later the whole length, from Radstock to Midford, was converted into a railway. Horses were used to haul wagons and at Midford Basin the coal was put on to barges.

By 1810 the Kennet and Avon Canal was fully open and a towing-path was also in use on the Avon Navigation between Bath and Bristol. The success of the Somerset Coal Canal can be judged by the fact that in 1812-13 over 66,000 tons of coal were transported along the canal, a figure which had risen to 138,000 tons by 1838.

It was not until 1854 that a railway seriously threatened the success of the canal. The Great Western Railway had opened its

Bristol to London line in 1841, competing directly with the Kennet and Avon Canal. The coal canal helped to keep it open with its coal traffic continuing down to the Avon at Bath or into north Wiltshire along the Wilts and Berks Canal. The broad gauge line which arrived at Radstock in 1854 was the beginning of the end and traffic on the canal began to decline. Eventually a railway opened between Bristol and Radstock and then the Somerset and Dorset Railway bought up the southern branch of the coal canal so that it could lay its extension to Bath along it. The canal traded at a loss in 1890 and the end came fairly quickly. It closed officially in 1898, after which the northern branch was also converted into a railway along much of its length by the GWR.

The Kennet and Avon, incidentally, was bought outright by the GWR in 1852, gradually declining until by 1910 all commercial traffic had more or less ceased.

Railways

The Wiltshire, Somerset and Weymouth Railway was promoted by directors of the Great Western Railway in the early 1840's. In 1844 it was also decided to build a branch from Frome to Radstock. After some difficulties the branch was opened by the GWR in November 1854 as a broad gauge single track line, eight-and-a-quarter miles long.

There were various plans to connect Radstock to Bath or Bristol and in 1863 the Bristol and North Somerset Railway was incorporated. As usual, there were financial difficulties, many of them caused by the company secretary, John Bingham. He was sentenced to 12 months imprisonment with hard labour for fraudulent dealings!

Although work had started on construction of the line it soon stopped and did not start again until 1870, when the Earl of Warwick took control of the finances. He owned several collieries around Clutton, as well as sawmills, quarries and brickworks. Work started again, but things did not go smoothly. In the winter of 1871-2 heavy rain caused landslides, and there was still the Pensford viaduct to build. This was the most expensive item on the line, with its 16 arches of 50-foot span, 995 feet long and 95 feet high. The line, between Bristol and Radstock and built to the standard gauge, was opened in 1873, and a year later the Radstock-Frome line was converted to the standard gauge, allowing trains to run from Bristol to Frome.

In 1882, the three-mile Camerton Branch opened from Hallatrow. This ran alongside or close to the Somerset Coal Canal, and its opening was the final blow for the canal company. In 1884, the GWR took complete control of the Bristol and North Somerset Railway, and in 1903 also bought the canal. A further eight miles of track were added to the Camerton Branch, making a link at Limpley Stoke with the Bristol to Westbury line. Most of the coal from Camerton and Dunkerton collieries then went by rail to sidings at Freshford, but very little passenger traffic used the line. In fact, there were no passenger trains after 1925, and the original three miles between Hallatrow and Camerton were taken up in 1930. Dunkerton pit closed in 1927, and after Camerton closed in 1950 there was little traffic left for the railway. It closed in 1951.

The 'main' line lasted a few more years, but passenger traffic ceased in 1959. Coal traffic continued between Radstock and Bristol – the mines supplied Portishead power station – but the line from Radstock to Mells Road was used less and less. When the Somerset and Dorset lines closed in 1966, a connection was made between them and the North Somerset line, so that coal from Writhlington, alongside the S & D to the east of Radstock, could be transported to Bristol. Back in 1871 the S & D had planned such a connection, but nothing had been done and the only way to transfer wagons from one railway company to another was through the sidings at Ludlows Colliery (closed in 1954).

In 1968, when only Writhlington and Kilmersdon pits remained open, an embankment north of Pensford was washed out and it was decided to close that section of the line, reopen the Radstock to Mells Road section, and transport coal via Frome and Westbury.

There was also a short branch from Mells Road to several collieries in the Nettlebridge Valley. The Westbury Iron Co. Ltd., which was formed in 1857, needed coal and limestone for its blast furnaces. A line was laid to the colliery at nearby Newbury, which the ironworks leased in 1858. The railway, generally referred to as the Newbury Railway, followed the course of the abandoned Dorset and Somerset Canal, and a few years ago one could still find remains of canal stonework next to lengths of iron rail in the fields. During construction, limestone was discovered at Vobster Cross, so the company also leased the land here, opening a quarry and building a limekiln.

The railway probably started operating in 1858 and at the same time a narrow gauge tramway was built to connect both Vobster Breach and Vobster collieries to the line via an incline. In 1867, Mackintosh Colliery, quarter of a mile to the west of Newbury, was opened and coal was sent from here to Newbury for transportation on the railway. Ironmaking soon declined at Westbury and in 1904 the railway, colliery and quarry were sold off. New owners continued to operate the railway and collieries, but only the quarry flourished, continuing to work until 1966, whereas the last of the pits to use the railway, Mells, closed in 1945.

A line was also laid from the GWR line to Bilbao quarry, a short distance to the east of the Newbury Railway, but in 1934 a siding was laid connecting the quarry to the Newbury Railway and this small line closed.

The Newbury Railway probably closed about the same time as Vobster quarry. For a while there was a siding connection to a bitumen terminal, and then to the ARC concrete pipe works, but then this connection was severed.

The complicated history of this railway is meticulously described in *The Newbury Railway* by Down and Warrington (Industrial Railway Society, 1979).

The Somerset and Dorset Railway opened its Bath extension from Evercreech Junction in 1874, allowing through traffic from Birmingham and Bristol to Bournemouth. The line followed the southern branch of the Somerset Coal Canal, the branch which had been converted into a tramway from Radstock to Midford. Soon after it was built, the railway was leased to the Midland and London and South Western Railways. In 1923, the newly formed Southern Railway and the London Midland and Scottish Railway legally became the owners of the line. From the 1930's, increasing road competition ensured that the railway made little money. In 1948, when British Railways was formed, the Southern Region became responsible for the line to Bath, but ten years later the Western Region took control. It has often been claimed that there was then a deliberate and unnecessary running down of the line. The Beeching Report in 1963 recommended closure, but it managed to struggle on till 1966.

As a post script to this section, it is interesting to note that between 1825 and 1917 at least 34 other schemes were proposed for building railways in the district, none of which were successful. These included the Bristol and English Channels Connection Railway, the Dover and Bristol Railway, the Radstock and Keynsham Railway and the Andover and Bristol Railway.

SOMERSET MINERS
IN CONVERSATION

As I walked along the paths and roads of North Somerset, I often met miners who had worked beneath the green fields in the blackness of the earth. I was struck by their friendliness, common sense, sense of humour and their enjoyment of life. They often had harsh words for some of their old managers, but they also appreciated and praised those who did their best for their men. They enjoyed talking about their days in the mine, and I could easily sense the pride they felt in being members of a select band of men.

I was reminded of D H Lawrence's essay, *Nottingham and the Mining Country*, written in 1929 where he says:

> 'The miners worked underground as a sort of intimate community, they knew each other practically naked, and with curious close intimacy, and the darkness and the underground remoteness of the pit 'stall', and the continual presence of danger, made the physical, instinctive, and intuitional contact between men, very highly developed, a contact almost as close as touch, very real and very powerful.'

From listening to what the Somerset miners said, I gained a much greater insight into what mining entailed, and how it affected the lives of the men and the community they lived in.

I hope that, as you read the following accounts, you will also get some of the feel of life in the coalfield.

Jack Gregory

Jack Gregory's father and four brothers were all miners and worked at Braysdown pit for most of their lives. He has always lived in or near Radstock, first at Woodborough Hill for thirty years, close to the colliery, and then, when he got married he moved to Waldegrave Terrace. He and his wife, Alice, wished to move nearer to Braysdown so they swapped houses with a couple who lived at Upper Whitelands, now demolished. Jack worked at Braysdown until it closed in 1959 and then worked at Kilmersdon for three years until he retired.

Jack started work at thirteen. He had to rise at about half past five and walk from Woodborough Hill to the pub on the Frome Road where the manager of the pit lived. When he arrived he cleaned boots, picked up coal and tidied the garden. He had to return to Braysdown at nine o'clock and he then called in at his home for breakfast. Sometimes he was given messages to take to Camerton pit. Every Saturday morning the manager's wife gave him a shilling.

At the pit he worked with his father and brothers at a face thirty yards long. One of his early memories is of having to wave a shovel backwards and forwards to produce enough air for his father's candle to burn. His father taught him how to use the guss and crook with which he had to pull his putt or sledge with its iron shoes. While he talked to me he crouched down on all fours to demonstrate how the guss fitted round his waist and the crook passed between his legs to hook on to the putt. Sometimes he had to crouch very low to get to and from the face - 'eighteen inches was good height so that was the little boys' job.' On his trousers his mother sewed little pads to protect his knees, although they had to be replaced every few days.

After it had been hauled in putts from the face to the road, the coal was put in larger wagons, usually on rails, and the older boys hauled these wagons perhaps half a mile to the main road. Pit ponies were then used to haul wagons to the shaft. Some of the faces were a mile away.

Quite often during the time he was talking to me, Jack would look back, almost in wonder, at what he had been through. 'Can't make nobody believe what we went through, you can't.'

The men who cut the coal at the face were the 'men', whereas the men who hauled the coal were the 'carting chaps', and the chaps could only become men after years of working with the wagons. The men got paid more and were paid by the tonnage of coal that came out. However, if they were working at a poor place, where there was little coal to be got, they got paid a fixed wage – a 'dead'un wage'. At one time this wage was seven shillings and sixpence a day and, for obvious reasons, was called the dog's licence. At a good place, though, men could earn a few shillings extra.

'I couldn't make you believe what we went through,' said Jack. He was a carting chap for over twenty years with his brothers. Some men were carting till they were well over forty years old, still wearing a guss at that age. Braysdown was the last pit to get rid of the guss and crook but Jack was reluctant to throw his away and sometimes when wagons came off the rails he found it easier to use the guss and crook rather than the lever they were expected to use. After its use had stopped, a rope was attached to both ends of the putt, the man at the face would fill it up and the chap would pull out the putt using the rope. When it had been emptied the man at the face would have to pull it back empty to the face.

At one time, the first load of coal sent up the shaft at the beginning of the shift was not counted as part of the miners' tonnage. This was because the miners had free coal. When I first interviewed Jack in 1986 he was still receiving free coal from the National Coal Board, about four tons a year.

Jack vividly remembers a fatal accident that occurred while the men were riding to the surface. One of the men killed was his neighbour whom he had always worked with. They both lived at Woodborough Hill, close to the pit, but they often had to run to the pit to be on time, sometimes in such a hurry that they had no time to do up their boots. They were full of life and full of fun, but one day, while ascending the shaft, the gate of the cage fell off. The cage had two decks, the top one holding six men and the bottom one eight. When they reached the top there were only five men on the bottom deck and they thought three men had fallen out. At the bottom of the shaft there was water, perhaps fifteen deep. (After the day shift was over, tanks were filled with this water, taken to the surface and emptied). The men who were waiting at the bottom for the cage to return heard the splashes and immediately dived in to get out the unfortunate men. Only two had fallen, but they were both dead. One had only a little mark across his forehead, and must have fallen straight down, but Jack's mate 'was all to pieces.'

Men were sometimes killed when the roof fell in. One cause of this was a 'belmo' or bell mould. Jack used this word to describe large pieces of rock embedded in the roof, shaped 'like a tree trunk', which would sometimes collapse, bringing down the roof with them.

There was never much trouble with water at Braysdown, the tanks in the cages apparently coping with much of what accumulated, but when Braysdown closed and Jack moved to Kilmersdon (or Haydon) pit, there was one face where water was 'dropping down like a flood all the time', and the men who worked there had to get oilskins before they went to it.

Before he moved, Jack had been working on the loader and now he was in charge of a bigger loader at Kilmersdon - 'The best job that I ever had.' A system of conveyor belts brought coal from the coalfaces and he had to see to the loading of the wagons. The boss was always pleased to see him because he kept the equipment clean. Every Saturday he worked for two hours cleaning off the loader and generally tidying up. The boss was a good one and sometimes Jack went with him to other pits underground. 'I went from Braysdown to Ludlows. You could go from Ludlows to Writhlington, Kilmersdon to Norton Hill.'

After nationalisation 'you wasn't drove so much' as under private enterprise, when the workers would always be on the lookout for the boss. Frank Beauchamp, who came to own many pits in the Radstock area, was a strict boss and would even pick up a little washer off the floor so that it would not be wasted. 'He wouldn't give away a halfpenny.'

The houses of Upper Whitelands where Jack lived were smaller than those at Lower Whitelands but were 'lovely' despite having outside toilets. There were a hundred yards of garden and he also looked after his neighbour's plot - 'I did it to keep mine clean' (of weeds). He had fifty or sixty ranks of strawberries and obviously loved gardening. Like many miners he kept pigeons and, with pride, showed me a photograph taken when one of his pigeons had won an important race. In the gardens there was never a weed (a fact already pointed out to me by other miners) and everybody except Jack seems to have kept a pig, which produced good manure for the garden - as well as meat.

'There was one woman out there, she said to Harry Nott ... now Harry did always talk through his nose ... haugh, haugh, haugh ... she said, 'Mr Nott, I got a pig down there and he isn't very well. I reckon he hasn't got a heart', so 'Haugh, haugh, haugh, I'll get rid of 'im.' So he got rid of 'im, killed 'im and cleaned 'im, took his heart out and put it in his pocket. Went up and said to the woman, 'You're right, your pig never had no heart.' He ate that heart himself.'

'All our family are buried at Writhlington. My uncle was the first buried over there, first through the gate on the left hand side.'

'I can't make you believe or anybody else believe ... I've seen pictures of slavery. They were no more slavery than what our jobs were, running about with no boots on. When I was in hospital my feet were black as ... I don't know, drainted into the skin. Three months after being in hospital all the black came off like a plate. After that I never went barefooted no more. I kept my boots on. You can say slavery.'

But this is also said with some pride and perhaps some nostalgia. Jack shows none of the bitterness that is readily apparent in, for example, A.F. Parfitt's account *My Life as a Somerset Miner*, which is worth reading.

Jack's account reminds me again of Lawrence's essay where he says of the collier: 'He roved the countryside ... prowling for a rabbit, for nests, for mushrooms, anything. He loved the countryside ... Very often, he loved his garden.' Jack said: 'I were a good poacher. I always had half a dozen pheasants hung up when I were at Tyning, and there were ducks along the stream.' And on one occasion, when Beauchamp's gamekeeper was ill in bed, Jack had to do his work for him or he would have got no pay.

I think that this picture that Jack gives is fairly typical of the North Somerset coalfield – the interrelationship of industry and countryside – and the good nature and good humour of the Somerset miner.

A.G. Church

Mr Church worked at Norton Hill colliery for 35 years, and at Kilmersdon for a few more years before he retired. After he retired he took up photography and he has a collection of over 3,000 photographs, many that he has taken himself, of the coalmines and the surrounding area. He has a great knowledge of the history of the coalfield and of the people who worked in it. Working in the mines before nationalisation showed him the inequalities there were in society, and he still feels bitter at times that, although life for most people nowadays is not as hard as it was in the twenties and thirties, there is still injustice.

During his time in the pits, Mr Church did many jobs. He used the guss and crook, drove pit ponies, and got out coal at the pit face and drove all kinds of machinery.

Some of his earliest memories of the pits are of the 1926 strike when he was in his teens: 'I remember A J Cook, a Somerset man, general secretary of the Miners' Federation of Great Britain, giving his speech to the miners at Radstock, and he was that exhausted he fell off the platform. He was a great man, similar to Arthur Scargill. People were more deprived than during the Scargill strike. I saw a boy go to school with a woman's pair of shoes that had the heels chopped off. I've seen boys at school with nothing on their feet. They carried their plates to school to go to the Salvation Army barracks for soup. The women used to dip a big iron ladle into this boiler. You had one cupful on the plate. This particular day I went with all the crowd to the barracks and this woman announced there wasn't enough soup for everyone, but there'd be some pudding with a bit of jam on top. So I had my plate of soup, and I thought to myself I'd be a bit cunning. I licked my plate clean and got in the queue to go up, and when I got there she looked at the plate. She said, 'What! Second helping?' They were terrible days.'

According to Mr church, Somerset was the most militant place in England. 'One miner tried to go to work (during a strike) and he got beaten up and that was the end of that.'

Mr Church's nephew was the fourth generation of a family that had worked at Kilmersdon colliery, and his father worked 52 years underground. Despite this , after the 1926 strike, his father, who was a militant, wasn't taken back on immediately. 'After four months there was a dangerous job at the pit, and then they sent for him. And you had to go, you know. My father said had he been a single man he wouldn't have gone, but it happened that when he completed this job that he got a job on the staff. I know of a miner who hadn't been employed after the strike for two years, and he used to get a few bob working on the farm. One day a man came knocking at the door and he had to go straight away to the pit to do the night shift.'

Mr Church believes that the decline of the coalfield started partly because of the change of ownership at the turn of the century. Although he does not agree with what was called the lord-of-the-manor system, these lords were better than the new men who took over. 'The Waldegraves built houses for their miners; they looked after their miners. The Beauchamps (the family which bought up many of the Waldegrave pits) never built anything. They took over the old collieries, salvaged what was any good, then closed the rest. They were terrible. I must have been underground only a matter of a few weeks, and when we stopped to have our food - we were allowed twenty minutes break, you sat down anywhere - this old chap, who lived in Lewis Beauchamp's house (brother to Sir Frank) started on about the Beauchamps. He said that all the Beauchamps were worth was a charge of shot (gunpowder). Beauchamp went to London and bought a shire foal, for £1,000 in those days, and when he came back it caught pneumonia and died. But he couldn't afford to let his daughter go and play tennis at Burnham. They were a terrible lot.'

Norton Hill pit was the most successful mine in Somerset. The seams of coal were thin, but they were economic, 'for the simple reason that the roof and the floor were so hard that very little timber was used and all the waste was packed behind like a cushion for the roof to rest on. But when mechanisation came in with hydraulic rams that would carry 70 tons each, all the back waste ground was allowed to break down into the old working.'

At this point, Mr Church drew a diagram to show how the seams of coal at Norton HIll had been severed by a fault, sometimes called the Great Overlap, in such a way that all the seams had been doubled. 'The middle seam was two foot – lovely coal; there was the Sly Vein – three foot nine to four foot; the New Vein – four foot; Big Vein – five foot; and the Globe – as high as this ceiling.'

I was talking to Mr church in front of a banked up coal fire. 'I think concessionary coal was what kept a lot of people in the pits – three hundredweight a week. That's Somerset coal that I've put on for your benefit, from 30 years ago. I've got loads down there in the shed – huge lumps. I've kept it in reserve.'

In the twenties and thirties the work force dwindled. 'After the war you had displaced persons from Europe, Poles, Italians, etcetera, but they weren't miners. Some would come here and work for a while, put a few bob together, then they'd go out and buy a fish shop.'

Like all the miners, Mr church had many memories of accidents. 'I saw a pretty few accidents. One man had his leg cut off with a coal cutter, and Len Church – no relation to me – he happened to be knowledgeable in first aid, he bound up the stump and saved his life. He never lost consciousness. He went back to work on top of the pit with a cork leg and a walking stick. I got away with my life a few times. I'll tell you one incident that happened. They used to allow you to come up half an hour early if you were going to a funeral or had some excuse, and this was the only occasion I asked to come up early. I got in the cage with the surveyor who happened to be there and as we passed the landing (where the cage stopped for coal to be loaded) 30 loads of coal ran away and came down the shaft, and we just missed that lot. That was a lucky escape. The wagons went down into the sump. It hindered the pit for half a day.'

On another occasion 'I was riding on a wagon. We used to have leather curtains across the road to divert the air. You weren't supposed to ride on the wagons, but at the end of the shift sometimes, if you had a sympathetic engine driver, he'd let you ride on them. And we'd duck our heads down as we'd ride through the curtains, sitting down in the wagons. On this particular day, I went to duck my head down, but I caught my head in a hole in the curtain and I nearly got strangled.'

In the days before nationalisation, men had to keep a check on how much coal they sent to the surface. 'Each man had his number. My number was twenty. You mixed up whiting in a pot. You used to have a piece of cane which you'd beat out with a hammer, to make a brush, and you'd mark your coal with whiting (ie by writing your number on the side of the wagon). The check-weigher at the top would know how much coal you had got out. They used to take a quart of water to make the whiting, but it was never enough, so they used to urinate in the pots.'

Mr Church was obviously a hard-working and skilful miner, and he told me of one particular day which bears this out. 'I'll tell you what I did. I should think it must have been something of a record. Two men and a chap were on one shift and I was on the opposite shift on my own – with a Scotchman. One afternoon I sent 22 loads of coal, which was one-and-a-half ton, single-handed. And I did it more or less to show those two other blokes who were on the other shift and, of course, the under-manager. When I came out he was standing there with his hands in his pockets and he said, 'How've you got on today?' I said, 'Twenty-two loads of coal today.' He said, 'What?' I said, 'I sent twenty-two loads of coal.' It happened like this: I was working in this road and it was one-and-a-half miles to get in there. Some people today, if they had to walk that distance would think they'd done a day's work. This chap said to me, 'Cliff

G. is the boss this afternoon; he don't like carrying gunpowder about. You go in and bore some holes. He'll fire them.' So I went in and bored five long six-foot holes, and when they went off, my God, there was a mountain of coal there, and all I had to do was load it. The chap – the Scotchman – was supposed to load the coal. He loaded the first and last, but I did the rest.'

Not every miner was necessarily a good miner. 'Different men had different skills (ie some men were more skilled than others at getting out the coal). Some men were as thick as a broom. All miners weren't good miners. You mustn't get that idea in your head – they weren't all good men. There were some very good miners – exceptional, but there were some very poor ones.'

All food that was taken down the pit had to be put in tins because of the mice. They went down the pit in the sacks of chaff for the pit ponies. Mr Church remembers the ponies being made redundant. 'The last ponies at Norton Hill had done 21 years underground. They were all well looked after. There was an ostler, a full-time man, who had a bit of overtime because he went in at weekends to feed them and clean them. The pit ponies seemed to live longer. One of them, Tom, lived till he was 40.'

He has talked to many people about the history of the area and has also read a great deal. 'I knew an old lady, Jane Withers, born in 1839. She had four miner sons and she died in 1935. She told me she rode from to Paulton to London on a coal barge. The barge was brushed clean down and the journey took fourteen days to go to Maida Vale and back. She said she'd wished it had lasted longer.'

Finally, Mr Church remembered how he used to cycle to Frome six days a week when he was younger. 'Norman Tebbit said his father got on his bike and looked for work. It took me bloody years to save up enough money to buy a bike.'

Howard Newth

(This is Howard's account of his life as he told it to me as I sat in front of his coal fire one cold February afternoon).
My grandfather is buried in Timsbury churchyard. He was 95 when he died and he was blacksmith at Grove pit. That shaft was filled in

just a few years ago. [It closed in 1878]. My father worked in the mines. He had three brothers and two of them worked in the mines. I had 30 years, mainly at Pensford, and I cycled there, seven miles there and seven back. On Saturdays I got up at 2.30, had my breakfast and started work just before 4.30. I started a bit before the men went down, getting coal for the boilers which were for the engine and electrical plant and engines for the inclines. In the week I got up about half-past-three to four. Once you started work you didn't stop. I started on the surface, putting the wagons in the cage. It was a continual run all the time, putting the empty ones in, pushing the loaded ones off. It was a single deck cage when I started, with two wagons one behind the other. It was a large shaft. You had to keep going all the time. Everything was recorded, any minutes lost were recorded and at the end of the day the manager wanted to know where those minutes were lost. You had to pull - I forget – about 140 loads an hour. If you only had 120 the manager wanted to know where those twenty had gone.

You had to keep going, rain or shine, with only twenty minutes for food. That was the only stop we had during the day. You started as soon as the hooter blew. There was no canteen. You sat down where you were with your food. If it was raining you got wet through. You were practically out in the open, with not much cover at all. If you got wet through going to work, you stayed in your wet clothes and worked like that and came home in them wet. Then when you came home your clothes had to be dried in front of your coal fire. As there were three coming home, the clothes would be all piled up on the hearth.

We only had a small cottage, two bedrooms, one room down with a little pantry place. We had to bath in front of the fire, where we had our food and everything. We just had a big saucepan on the fire and a little tin bath. You knelt down, washed the top part, then wiped the top, then you slipped your trousers down. If there was anyone about they'd come and wash your back. If there wasn't anyone about and someone came to the door, then, 'Mind washing my back?' You imagine having three to do. I used to try and get there first and use the clean water. You didn't change the water all the time. It took a long time to boil up a saucepan. You didn't have electric then, only oil lamps in the house. A married person got three hundredweight of coal a week, which was ample really. It was big fires in those days. You had no double-glazing and there was plenty of room for a draught to come under the door that blew you nearly away sometimes. We had stone floors and you didn't have carpet in those days, just a piece of coconut matting.

The floors were often washed over and the grate was black-leaded. Toast in front of the fire was lovely and if you cooked a goose – you didn't often get one, you were too poor to buy one – you'd hang it in front of the fire on the jack. You'd wind it up and it would keep turning. You did herrings in front of the fire and bloaters. As children, for breakfast perhaps it would be – put some bread in a basin, pour some boiling water on, then soon as you put it on, tip the water away. Then put some milk and sugar on that. We used to call it sop, or you had a bit of porridge.

I started work delivering newspapers. I used to go from here [Timsbury] to Hallatrow to pick the papers up, meet the train at half-past-seven in the morning, come back and deliver them – five shillings a week.

I tried down the pit when I was sixteen. The manager said to me, 'You be too old, me son, you be too old.' That's because when you were sixteen you started paying unemployment insurance which was only threepence or sixpence, but they wanted you before they had to start paying that. That was at Camerton. So then I went to the Star Hotel in Wells to work - £1 a week, live in, half a day off once a week. I used to cycle up home, then leave home at eleven o'clock and get down there just as the cathedral clock was striking twelve. Perhaps you wouldn't see a soul all the way; on a pushbike with a carbide lamp or perhaps an oil lamp.

Then I happened to go to Pensford with another lad. I said I'd never go in the pit, but the manager said, 'I can give both of you a start,' so I accepted and stayed there 30 years. We weren't unhappy, mind. We accepted that we had nothing else. All this village really were miners. There were four or five pits in this village and Camerton. I was a labourer really, but sometimes I took on banksman. That's someone operating the cage.

There were no baths then. Pensford pit had the first ones in Somerset, but some of the men didn't take to it much because they didn't like to expose themselves.

Your wife or mother would always worry if you were late coming home, always worrying that something had happened, that you'd met with an accident. That was common. You got explosions or roof falls causing broken arms, or some were killed with roof falls. Perhaps the wagons would break away. The cage came down on top of one of the men in our pit one day – killed him. And many years ago one man fell out the cage going down and there happened to be a manhole down the side of the shaft. He fell in that one and when they went down to pick up the pieces, the old man shouted out, 'Let's have some jumpin' light!' He was lucky he fell in this place.

Bromley was open at that time. It closed just before Pensford. That had a very small shaft. To get a horse down there, it had to be trussed up like a chicken for the oven. They put it in a net and hung it under the cage and let it down, but in our shaft you could drive a horse straight in the shaft. They went at speed. At Upper Conygre [in Timsbury] it was very slow. You could walk along the road and back before it came up.

My father worked at Pensford. He used to walk there when they were sinking it – a long walk, but he lived to 95, and my wife's grandmother, she lived to 95.

Wages were low, four shillings and elevenpence a day, but in summer you often didn't work because there was no sale for the coal. You had the day off, but you weren't paid for it and we weren't paid for bank holidays. We had no holidays and we worked six days a week until it changed during the war. If we worked only three days a week we were better off than if we worked four because we got three days unemployment pay. We had to go to the unemployment exchange and sign on every day we weren't working. It was only a wash-house place down Temple Cloud. You had to wait there in the queue and when you got up to the man perhaps he'd say, 'I'm gonna have my dinner now.' Or he might say, 'Take your hat off.' But who was he? Why should we show any more respect to him? He was only a working man like us. And then he had to know if you'd been genuinely seeking work! You had a job, you were on short time and you had to give a list of where you'd been looking for work. Then if you worked four days, you didn't get any dole.

My mother and father had no employment money. They had to manage without it. They had to have time off in winter sometimes because they couldn't get the coal away when the canal was frozen over and the roads were too slippery.

About here there were two pits, Braysdown and Camerton. Well, you had to listen to the steam hooter at half-past-ten at night to know if there was any work next day, three hoots for Camerton and five for Braysdown.

It was hard times up to the time I was married about '35 or '36.

I worked on top for a few years at Pensford, then went underground. I had various jobs, sometimes sending coal up the pit, sometimes taking wagons away, sometimes riding the journey [looking after wagons as they made their way into the mine workings by standing on the continuous rope which was guided over metal rollers between the rails, and holding on the wagon]. Sometimes I had to see to the pumps. Pensford got flooded twice. When they went down deeper with the shaft, they broke into the water and it flooded the shaft. They tried tipping lots of clay down and filling it up, so they could work the seams at the upper levels, but it didn't stop the water completely. Then they pumped it out and abandoned the deep workings.

They had to keep the pumps going continuously. Eventually they wanted to go down deep because those seams were the Bromley seams. They drove an incline down at one in three, cutting strata all the way. When they tapped the water, they pumped cement in, sealing the water as they went through until they touched the

Bromley seams. It was very expensive, and the seams were not very good. It was very dirty coal and they had a job to sell it. If you had a two-foot seam you had a good one. But it was difficult working on a seam that size. It was a case of guss and crook. Machines weren't really suitable for these small seams, and you had so many faults. It was never a profitable pit, really.

Once when I was working up the top the gates got stuck up. The cage brings the gates up. It'd got arms sticking out which lifted the gate. I used to put the wagons on. I'd collect them and put them on the 'stricking plate' [a metal plate by the side of the shaft on which wagons could be swivelled round into the cage]. I whipped them round on the plate and they went in over the pit because the gate hadn't come down when the cage went down the shaft. It had got stuck up with tar or dirt somehow or other. Well, I went up to the manager and he said, 'That silly bugger been and shoved the wagons down the pit!' They rattled down. At the bottom of the pit they had some big railway sleepers across. They smashed through them and down into the deep.

You come to think of the remarkable amount of weight on that headgear, eight steel ropes (four to each cage), plus the weight of the cage, and several tons of load. One day we had the case of an engine driver who over-wound. He went too high. Usually there was a thing that puts the brake on, but it didn't work. Those poor devils going down had their legs broken. Twelve injured but none killed. The safety device didn't happen to work that day. But that was a monotonous job, driving the engine all the time, going up and down.

You used to have a candle in your hat. At first it was tallow candles with lots of threads to make a wick, then oil lamps, then wax candles. You put it in your hat [in a special candle holder]. When a lady threw her hat out, we had the hat, cut the brim off, stuck a piece of leather on the front and stuck the candle holder in there – a felt hat. They didn't supply you with anything down there. Then we had carbide lamps. You had a little tin in the morning, a tin full of carbide, from the candle house, and that lasted you through. There were never electric lights at Pensford. The explosions years ago were caused by coal dust. What they used to do was throw stone dust or flue dust. That may be your job when you started. You went down the roads throwing this dust up and around everywhere and that dust neutralised the coal dust.

I always remember as a boy, mother said to us, 'Father hasn't come home.' We got frightened. 'We shall have to go and look for him.' He was on afternoons, and should have been home about ten o'clock. We had to go down to Camerton to see what had happened. We decided to go and call on one of the banksmen. He worked on the top and counted the men up. He must be accurate, but somehow or other he missed father. He said, 'I'm sure I said good-night to him, but we'll go down and see.' So we went down. He'd been left down there. He was working in a place with bad air and, of course, your candles don't burn so freely then. That's how he tells his time, his candles burning, near enough, and when he came to the pit bottom there was no one there. They'd all gone home, and there was no way of getting out, not until the morning. Although you could communicate with the top, there was no one to communicate with. The stoker had gone home, the engine men were gone home. Father was down there by himself. He'd been working away from the other workers, you see. So we had to go and get the stoker out, go and get the engine driver out, one to get up steam, the other to drive the engines.

You had to bite your tongue in those days. If you said anything – 'You go on up, me sonny' [i.e. you're sacked]. You mustn't answer back.

Towards the last I did leave Pensford for a few weeks and went to Camerton New pit. I was working at the bottom of an incline, what they call hitching up. I had to hitch loads at the bottom and send them up. There was a single rope with an engine pulling it up. Once when the empties came down they toppled over on their sides all across the road. The boss came down and shouted, 'What the devil's the matter, Howard?' ''Ere,' I said, 'what's the matter with you?' 'Well, they're up there waiting.' At that I put my coat on and sat down. I said to him, 'Thee can put it on, Albert!' [ie put the coal back in the wagons]. He replied, 'I didn't mean it like that, Howard.' He never frightened me; I stood up for myself. 'Don't blame me, then,' I said. I couldn't have cared if he'd sent me up straightaway then [sacked him] which some would. He was as nice as pie afterwards. 'I'm not going to be talked to like an animal. You don't frighten me, Albert,' I thought. That's how they treated us, and it was time someone stood up.

The unions didn't do much in those days. The coal owners had the money; they could beat us every time. When we struck that time in 1921, it was only because they were going to take off a penny a day. That was a nine months' strike, and we didn't know where to turn for money. My mother, she almost cried, she had no money. We had two shillings a week distress money, and then you had to get rid of everything you could, go and catch a few rabbits, and you lived off the vegetables out of the garden, or have it on tick. A lot of the shops trusted you, hoping they'd get it back when you were back at work. I saw my mother with the last sovereign. She let the lady in the shop have it and she said, 'You can have it back again when you can afford it.' My mother wanted to keep that sovereign. In fact, we've still got it now.

It was hard for mother. Look at these grates - cleaning all these grates; and the washing, in a shed in the garden somewhere. And the toilet was at the bottom of the garden. You had a bucket to tip. Not a very pleasant job, was it? The toilet door didn't come to the bottom nor to the top, so you had plenty of draught blowing in. We had a heap where we put our ashes. We dug down a bit, put the ashes there, tipped the bucket over it, then tipped some more ashes on top. After some time that did accumulate, you see. We had to load it up in the wheelbarrow and wheel it away out into the allotments, 1,000 yards away or more. We put it on the allotment or the garden. Of course, it smelt pretty high, mind. Everybody had to do that. There was no drainage, you see. There was no refuse collection either. We took it to the quarries, but we didn't have so many tins then.

Sometimes the colliers kept a pig. They ate up scraps, potato peelings. Then you killed the pig at home. As kids we used to say, 'Can we have the bladder?' We tipped the water out, the pig's water, and blew it up. We'd think no more about it. A football, that was. Then you cut the hooves off and put them on your fingers. It was rather fun when you killed a pig. The man who killed the pig, he had a special round ball on the end of a stick with a handle on it, and there was a spike sticking out of that ball. He would swing it round so it would stick in the pig's head, then he would get down and slit his throat. He'd miss sometimes, mind. Then you had to burn the pig, burn the hair off and scrub him down and when you had the bacon you'd hang it up on the stairs. That was the highest part. You had a hook up there, tie the bacon up there and cut a piece off when you wanted it. That would keep. Wives used to make faggots with some of the liver and that.

Most people kept a few hens, and we used to pick acorns in the winter. Threepence a peck, I think it was. Farmers used to buy them off us for pigs.

My father used to walk to Bristol on Sundays when he was courting. She was working in service there. They [those in service] were treated almost like animals nearly. They used to put you up in the attic. But some were good. There were some devils, mind. Over at Stanton Prior a person [in service] had her daughter named the same as the Earl's daughter. They turned them out of the house.

My grandfather got sacked for taking some drink up to the colliery here in the village. He didn't know what to do and he had a big family, so he went selling tea down around Compton Dando. He had bags of tea hanging down over his shoulder. That didn't pay, so the men got together, collecting, and gave him a horse and cart. So he went hauling coal after that, and he did very well. But that same man that reported him [to the boss], when he was going to school – he had a young boy – he got killed on the corner by the pit, on the crossroads. They were in a motorbike and sidecar, and a car drove into them. Both of them were killed. We were kids and saw them. We thought they were sleeping. They were unconscious and we told grandfather, and he said, 'I'd'a forgive, but I don't forget.' He said he'd have his day.

For the miner there was no recreation. You had a bit of football, watching or playing, but your only other bit of recreation was gardening. You had so much garden to do, you see, but they'd never touch it on a Sunday. Yet they got it done. My aunts would never carry a bucket on a Sunday. You should never cut a cabbage on a Sunday, and if we started running around on a Sunday my mother would say, 'Enough of that today. I don't want you running round today. 'Tis Sunday today.' And I used to play the piano a little bit and mother would say if I tried to play a song, 'Enough of that.' I could play hymns from morning to night, but I mustn't play anything else. Mind, I must say they were peaceful Sundays!

We didn't know any difference, I suppose. We accepted our life. I've enjoyed my life whatever I did, although perhaps some of it wasn't altogether to my liking. I enjoyed myself in the pit. I had a bit of fun as well, because it was our life. Looking back now, I don't think you would enjoy it now. I can't see that anyone would wear a guss and crook in these days. They wouldn't do it.

'Twas slavery, really. Because I've known the manager come along, Joe Smith, I've seen him stay on the pit all day, watching to see everything kept moving, looking at his watch. You were treated like animals in a way.

I suppose the manager, in later years, wasn't bad. He frightened them all, mind. They used to jump, and it shouldn't be like that, should it? I went to Fry's [the chocolate factory at Keynsham] for sixteen years afterwards, and I found the miners were more united. They helped one another more than the workers in Fry's would. I used to tell them at Fry's what a soft job they had. 'They could get rid of half of you and you wouldn't be missed.' They thought they were going to have this easy money for evermore.

Miners would do anything for you. You had your ups and downs, I know, but if you were ill, they'd bring things in for you. You could go to bed and leave the door unlocked. You'd go into a neighbour's house: 'Like a bit of fried tater tonight?' they'd ask. Well, that was good, a little bit of fried potato and fried cabbage. Meat was fairly cheap. We used to go to Radstock on a Saturday night. That market was on to about ten o'clock at night or gone. When it was late you got meat cheap because they had no fridge to put it in. You didn't say then, 'Don't eat the fat!' We liked the fat and a nice bit of dripping. You had a nice piece of bread and dripping, it was lovely. Or lard. We bought what we called 'flic' and melted that down. Pure lard that was. That was lovely, bread and lard with a bit of salt on it. We used to grease the wheelbarrow with it, too. I can see the white going round on the wheel now.

We used to walk to Radstock. We walked everywhere. My father never rode a bike in his life. He walked everywhere, really; he was pretty strong. I've known him when he was well over 80 go off with four hundredweight of potatoes on a wheelbarrow,then stack them up...

(My interview with Howard finished there. His close friend arrived to discuss the local footpaths. When I met Howard again, thirteen years after the first edition of this book, he still seemed as active as he had been in 1986. For many years, Howard and two friends have been walking and surveying the paths, not only of Camerton, but also of many other parishes. They record everything about the paths for the local council, so that obstructions can be removed, stiles renovated and bridges repaired. They call themselves the Timsbury Ramblers and, at one time, used to lead a party of locals on a walking trip around the lesser known points of interest in the parish. Walkers in North Somerset owe him and his friends a great deal).

George

George comes from Frampton Cotterell, north of Bristol. Although his father was not a miner, his grandfather was and he had other relations who worked in the mines. One uncle, for example, worked first in a mine at Coalpit Heath and when that closed went to Pensford colliery.

When the Second World War started, George worked in Yate at an aircraft factory which eventually moved to Temple Cloud, and it was here he met his future wife. After serving in the Army as a vehicle mechanic and after several jobs, he went to the training school at Old Mills pit. He decided to work in the pits mainly because the pay was so good, about £10 a week, compared with the £6 a week he was earning elsewhere. There was also the opportunity to work overtime at weekends and another bonus was the free coal. The allowance then was ten hundredweight a month. He worked first at New Rock, then at Old Mills, spending about ten years in the pits.

George and his wife have always lived in a small village south of Farrington Gurney and after his training he cycled across to New Rock pit which is a stone's throw from Downside Abbey, a landmark for miles around. He would have preferred to work at Old Mills because it was a more modern pit with its coal cutting machinery etc., but there were no opportunities to do so at the time. Unfortunately, not long after starting work underground, he had an accident. He was riding on the front of a wagon as it was being hauled underground. At one point the roof was very low, he must have raised his head or stood up, and he was dragged back over the top of the wagons, injuring his side and legs. He had to have several stitches in his wounds, but was back at work within a fortnight.

At the bottom of the shaft was a system of endless ropes, continually moving along, to which trains of empty wagons were connected. They were pulled to a turnout – a kind of parking place – where they were unclipped. Men then pushed them back to the face workings where they were once again clipped to the rope to be hauled back to the shaft. George's first job was riding the endless rope, ie being responsible for the train of wagons travelling to and from the turnouts. He had to ride on a seat on the front wagon, clip it to the rope and unclip it when it reached its destination.

George's next job was 'running the road'. Close to the coalface there were metal pans (large troughs) into which coal was shovelled. As the seams were steep the coal would shoot down the pans which opened into the road at the bottom. A board or trap stopped it spilling on to the roads and George had to push empty wagons to different chutes, load up and then push them back out to join a train of loaded wagons. He explained that in certain places there were inclines where the wagons had to be pulled up the 'haulage' from one level to another by rope which was operated by an engine at the top. If for any reason the wagons had to be stopped part of the way up the incline a drag on the wagons would act as a brake. This was a metal bar, or spike, which would dig into the ground like an anchor. Sometimes the wagons ran freely along the rails and when they needed to be brought to a halt a man would shove a 'sprig' – an iron bar with a handle – into the wheels to slow them down and bring them expertly to a halt at the right place.

Some of the coal seams were large, but they might consist of two or three feet of coal, two feet of muck (the 'gob' or rubbish) and a further one foot of coal on top. Very often there was much dirt in the coal seams.

At New Rock the seams were so steep that if a miner put his tools down they would start to roll away. Also it was very warm underground and the system of mining old-fashioned, with very little machinery, and roofs supported entirely by timber props. Old Mills on the other hand had hydraulic props and a mechanical system of coal cutting. George discussed his situation with his father-in-law, also a miner, who put in a good word for him with the under-manager at Old Mills. Consequently, he started work there, at first on the night shift. Eventually, he was working at the face, not getting the coal, but 'flitting'. To explain what this involved, George described the system of working at the face.

The main road, down which the coal was taken in wagons back to the shaft, was ten feet high and its roof was supported by iron rings. This road was driven, or cut out, ahead of the seam which was at right angles. Parallel to the main road, perhaps a hundred yards away, was another road, the airway, essential for the circulation of fresh air. Ventilation fans were always operating to ensure this. The first stage in getting the coal was running the cutting machine along the face. This was driven by a motor, set in the road, and was about four feet long, on wheels, with a jib about three and a half feet long on which were cutting teeth set at different angles. One man drove this machine, starting from the airway, all along the seam to the road. This machine cut into the base of the coal seam to a depth of about three feet and cut a thickness of about four to six inches (so that when it had finished its work there would be a four to six inch gap at the bottom of the seam, going in about three feet). Behind the cutter was a man, or men, timbering up, putting posts and other wood to hold up the roof. The cutter left behind it big piles of cuttings, but the big 'nub' of the coal seam would still stay still. Men then shovelled in under the seam and got out as much of 'the gummings' as they could. With luck the coal would then drop so that it could be shovelled up. If it did not drop it was necessary to use explosive. Usually holes would be bored into the seam before cutting started and shots of explosive were placed in them and fired by a pit deputy. The coal was shovelled on to a conveyor system, which was either a continuous belt or metal pan which had a continuous chain dragging coal along it. When this was done, the pans were 'flitted' over, ie moved forward, nearer to the face, and the cutting could start again, deeper into the seam. All the time, props were being put up to support the roof, but as the men moved forward the supports were removed and gradually the roof behind them would collapse to the floor.

This job, flitting, was one that George enjoyed, but near the end of his time at Old Mills there were problems with water, which sometimes poured like a flood through the roof. Men had to work in mackintoshes and occasionally they were allowed to finish their shift early, because they were soaking wet. Another problem, one common to all the mines, was faulting. It might be possible to find the seam again, but sometimes it would be lost. Or a face might be of a good thickness, perhaps three or four feet, and then, after it had been worked for, say, a hundred yards, it might become so thin that it was uneconomic to mine.

One day George called in at Clarks factory and applied successfully for a job. He knew Old Mills would soon close and he wanted a change from getting wet underground.

Looking back on his time in the pits, George said, 'Although I worked underground, I enjoyed working down there, because there was a spirit, there was a system… There's a marvellous butty system; your butty is your mate.' Everyone knew his life depended on his fellow workers and this knowledge bred a closeness which George found lacking in most other jobs he had.

George's wife also has close connections with the mines. Her grandfather worked at Old Farrington pit and her grandmother had shares in Farrington Level or Marsh Lane (see Walk 6). Her father first worked at Moorewood Colliery. She remembers him talking about the pit ponies, one of which was called Nelson. Her father was the eldest of thirteen children and left school at the age of twelve to start work in the mine. During the First World War the story is that the miners drew lots to see who should join up and who should stay. Later he went to Bromley pit, near Pensford, and then New Rock, cycling to work every day. In wet weather he would put sacks over the handlebars and across his knees to protect himself. In the dark he would also use his miners' carbide lamp as well as his cycle lamps to light his way. He never bathed at the pits. At first, of course, there were no baths, but even after they had been installed he preferred to cycle home and get into the tin bath in front of the fire. George's wife, when she was at junior school, was never met by her mother at the school gates. That was the time when her father came home and her mother had to have the water hot for his bath. One day he knocked the top of his little finger off at work and he and his wife were in a panic – because miners received no pay if they could not go to work. Although miners paid a little money into a friendly society every week, what was paid out was hardly enough to live on.

Unfortunately, he had problems with his health. He developed diabetes and had to retire early because of trouble with his breathing, not caused by silicosis however. He retired just before he was 65 and received a pension of £2 a week, as well as an allowance of coal. He did not live to enjoy a long retirement. He died at the age of 67 and his widow then received a pension of £1 a week.

Alex Hann

I interviewed Alex in the building which once was the bath house of Ludlows pit and in which he now has his office. As we talked we looked out across the centre of Radstock, the church and its school on our left which was on the other side of the railway line, and the chimney of Middle Pit to our right (now demolished). He knows a great deal about the pits in Somerset and the people who worked in them, but in this interview I concentrated mainly on finding out about his life and how it was affected by his association with the mines.

Alex's grandfather and his uncles worked in the local pits, but his parents were not keen for him to work in them. He was told continually to stay out of them. Part of the reason for this was that his grandfather had been killed at the bottom of the shaft at Ludlows. The top of the shaft was just a few yards from where we were talking. He left seven or eight children and this event obviously left a bit of a shadow as far as the coal mines were concerned. Alex's father was eleven at the time, and when he reached the age of 21 he was awarded £26 compensation.

Alex started his education at the church school when he was three, in the 1920s.

'In this area in those days, the thing that was important was education. If you were bright enough you could go on to further education, but you had to prove you were, so this meant a scholarship examination to get to secondary school. I took this exam in the church school. It was pretty certain that only about one in ten would pass and one of the early pieces of sheer excitement I had as a boy was taking home my obviously successful testimonial from school to say I'd passed. Until then we were regarded as rather wayward material and I think my mum probably shed a few tears because this was going to make a lot of difference. I did know that my parents, especially mother, were keen that we [he and his twin brother] succeeded, so it was a double reward for them - and double cost because sending a boy to secondary school meant a lot of expense. We had to have a bicycle, which was £4.10s. in those days, to travel to school, and also that was one of the badges of success – a new bike. I remember running home breathless with the results of that examination. The envelope was sealed, but the headmaster had whispered in our ears, 'Well done!' He was an ex-captain of the First World War who lived in the school – a strict disciplinarian.'

Those children who did not pass stayed on at the primary school until they were fourteen. Alex remembers, not unnaturally, feeling a little bit superior when he passed the exam, but he was only separated from those who did not pass when he was at school, and at weekends 'you still played with your old friends.'

The school, which was conveniently close to Midsomer Norton station on the Somerset and Dorset line, took children from a wide area, from Coleford and Oakhill in the south, and from Temple Cloud, Clutton and Peasdown St John in the north. As there were no school buses in those days, before the Second World War, children either had to walk, go by train or cycle.

Alex was at this school from 1935 to 1939. Then the war started. A grammar school in London was evacuated to his school and it was filled to overflowing with pupils and teachers. He had already joined the ATC, but because he was not old enough to join up, when he left school he went to work in an armaments factory in Paulton. This was owned and run by a firm called Simmons. Its trading name was Aerocessories, short for aircraft accessories. It had moved from Brentford and it was the first time Alex had come into contact with modern industry.

'We were used to peering into the blacksmith's shop, looking at the fire and soot, the blacksmith's great beefy arms, his waistcoats and tobacco tins, but this was quite a different affair. There were huge, wide-open floor areas, brilliantly lit, glistening, flashing machines and men in white coats. It looked like a laboratory. So I thought there must be something about this worth learning. It hit me very forcibly.'

He started work at a wage of sixpence-halfpenny an hour, twelve hours a day, from eight till eight. He learnt a great deal from this experience: 'Many of the things I do now have got roots in what I learnt there.' He did well at the factory, working his way up to a position of responsibility and then, after two years, he joined the Royal Air Force.

'Off I went to report at Lord's Cricket Ground in London. Because I'd had training in a factory and knew a good bit about precision engineering, I was told there was room for me in the technical branch of the RAF. After learning how to march about and shoot, I was sent to Blackpool to a trade-test board, and I did extremely well. I was then sent off on a course of technical training. This course was in Melksham in Wiltshire, not far from my home. I remember distinctly getting down to the station in Bath. Although I enjoyed the RAF and would do it all again, I was always homesick. So I rang the labour exchange in Radstock where my dad was working. I said, 'Dad, Alex here.' He replied, 'Good Lord!' and in true Somerset style asked,

'Where bis to?' 'Bath station.' 'Where be goin'?' 'Melksham. I shall be home this weekend.' This was delightful.'

Alex went to the Far East and served with the Third Tactical Air Force with the Fourteenth Army. He travelled to such places as Bombay and Calcutta, and followed the army down through Burma to Rangoon.

'It was fantastic, really. I can remember seeing Mount Everest in the distance from Assam. And the tea they grew there, you could smell it for miles.'

When he returned after the war in 1947, he thought he had had enough of travelling. 'I felt I'd done pretty well everything and been everywhere, and so I said, I'm going nowhere else. This is good enough for me, and the only job around here was either to work on the farm or in the pits.'

But times had changed. The mines were being nationalised, and now there was a proper career structure. 'So much to everybody's surprise, I joined the NCB.'

About 60 men started at the same time as Alex did, about 70 percent being ex-servicemen. There was little else for them to do at that time. 'We had electricians, craftsmen of all sorts, who could go into these trades in the mines. And then the Mining Institute was started in 1948 at Old Mills, where all the training was done from then on in this area. It remained there for over ten years, before it moved to what became Norton-Radstock Technical College.'

The way up was a difficult one, and many dropped out before reaching the top.

'I found that the way onwards could take two routes - you could either take a degree at university, backed by the NCB, or do it more slowly, but ending up with similar qualification. It would take a year longer, but you wouldn't have to go away from home. That was important. Also, we were a bit old for university, at 23 or 24. It was a bit like going back to school. So I chose the second way, which allowed me to stay at home in the area. It started as a class of 60, but after about four years there were only fifteen of us left. And that fifteen dropped down to about seven and only two of us out of that seven ever qualified in mine management. The others worked in the mines, but did not stay on to qualify. It was arduous and I had to do work in all aspects of mining. For example, I would spend a few months in the blacksmith's shop, then the electrician's shop, then I'd be in the shaft working. The men accepted you, but they'd give you a hard time to go with it. You wouldn't get away with not doing anything. They'd never been used to wasting their time, and they weren't going to let you waste yours. They were all disciplined.'

To begin with, Alex, although training for management, was, in his own words, 'a very lowly miner.'

'When you started, you were the boy, and if you said anything too much you'd get a bunch of fives in your mouth, so you learnt to keep your mouth shut and know your place. Discipline in the mine has to be very strict. The man who issues the orders has to be obeyed. The men were strong and used to the work; they were attuned to it, having done it all their lives. We got a little more acceptance because we'd been in the armed forces and served during the war, and there were still quite a few people, very good friends of mine, who had served in the First World War, so we had something in common.'

During his training, Alex spent one day a week at the Mining Institute. Every year there were exams and if you were not good enough you had to leave the course.

'I remember in '49, '50 and '51, I had the best results and was granted a three-week course at Swansea University College, so instead of going on holiday with the rest of the boys, I went to school instead. I joined all the boys from the valleys in the university and went to the lectures. There must have been about 200 of us there from everywhere in the South Wales area, but only one, or sometimes two, from Somerset. All the mining exams were held in Cardiff and after ten years I qualified as a mine manager. It was an important day in my life when I was informed by the Ministry of Fuel and Power that I had received a First Class Certificate of Competency to Manage a Mine.'

During this time, Alex had begun to specialise in mining rescue. In 1953 he was appointed to the Miners' Rescue Station for Somerset and Bristol, as assistant to the superintendent. This station was responsible for the training of rescue teams, equipping them, fire-fighting, etc. In 1961 he was appointed as the Superintendent of Mines Rescue. This meant that he was now responsible for this aspect of mining throughout Somerset. A few years later he was elected as secretary of the mines rescue service for the whole of the United Kingdom. He held this position for ten years, during which time he travelled all over the country, arranging conferences, writing papers, giving talks, inspecting pits, investigating accidents, etc. He was also closely involved in activities in South Wales.

'If they had an explosion or fire over there, they'd send for us, so we might have to go to a mine we'd never heard of before, on, say a Sunday afternoon. The times I've had to go off in the snow, say goodbye to the wife, drive 80 miles to Wales, then bunk down with a couple of blankets for some rest in between shifts.'

Then, in 1973, the last mines in Somerset closed.

'By the time that happened, I'd built up all this experience and I was 50 years old. So the board said they'd like me to apply for half a dozen jobs they were interested in taking me on. But I said, 'I've got children at school, I'm not going away from here. I understand you pension people off at 50. I'd prefer to choose that. So at 50 I retired from the board on a pension, then I started my own consultancy here in Radstock. I bought up Ludlows site, improved the site to make workshops, and made an office in the bath house.'

Alex also worked for many years in Cornwall in tin mining after leaving the coal industry and with his sons now runs a thriving business as well running a wide variety of courses for people in such areas as the construction and water industries, wherever workers have to go into tunnels, wells etc.

Alex considers himself to have been privileged to have worked in the mines.

'I consider I made a success of my career. I worked hard, but we were never brought up for anything else. I never grew up with high expectations. I knew I would only get what I worked and studied for.'

Opposite: Stile near Lower Writhlington, made by Evans' Foundry. Note WPC – Writhlington Parish Council – on left-hand post.

The Walks

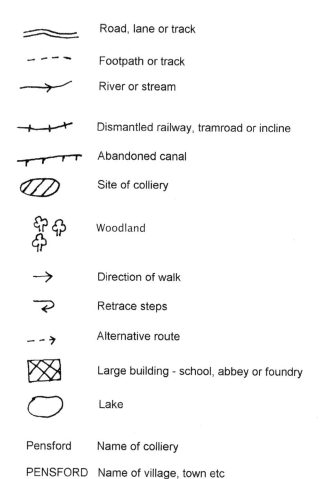

Road, lane or track

Footpath or track

River or stream

Dismantled railway, tramroad or incline

Abandoned canal

Site of colliery

Woodland

Direction of walk

Retrace steps

Alternative route

Large building - school, abbey or foundry

Lake

Pensford   Name of colliery

PENSFORD   Name of village, town etc

Key to Sketch maps

1   Pensford and Bromley

Distance: 4.5 miles
Starting Point: Rising Sun public house, Pensford
Map Reference: 618637

The walk first follows the River Chew, then climbs up the side of the valley towards Bromley colliery, before descending to Salter's Brook, beneath the imposing batch of Pensford colliery. This is an easy walk to follow, but the descent of Pensford colliery batch is still difficult in places. Fortunately, it was being cleared and steps were being put in when I last walked here.

The village of Pensford is bisected by the busy A37 Bristol to Shepton Mallet road, but on the old road, which crosses the River Chew by a medieval bridge, there is hardly any traffic, and there is plenty to look at. Downstream you can see the modern road bridge; the previous one was swept away in the floods of 1968, although the medieval bridge stayed firm. On the house across from the war memorial is a plaque which shows the flood level, and there is a similar one on a building near to the pub, the Rising Sun. On the main road, on the western side of the modern bridge, is the building which once housed the Pensford Miners' Welfare Institute.

The church was not used after the floods and for a time was an exhibition centre. Signs outside suggest that it is now unsafe.

Beyond the church is the railway viaduct which dominates this part of the village. It carried the BNSR on its way from Bristol to Frome. It was built in 1873 and has 16 arches, with brown and grey stone and brick arches. *Kelly's Directory* of 1875 says: 'Here is a viaduct on the North Somerset Railway, over a quarter of a mile long, 100 feet high, spanning an immense valley, and is one of the finest structures of its kind in the west of England.'

To the right of the entrance to the Rising Sun car park is a lane

75

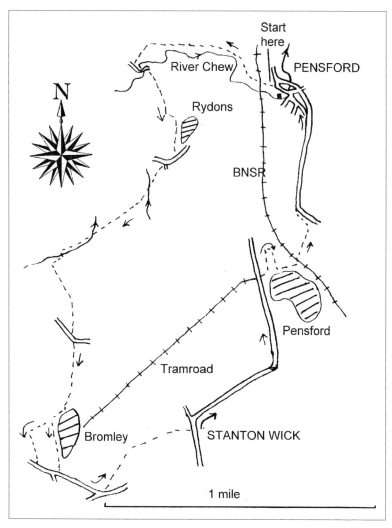

which rises up and leads towards the viaduct. Follow this lane, under
the viaduct to a wooden kissing gate where there is a notice
welcoming you to walk in Culvery Wood. Walk on down the hill to
where there is a stile close to the river. Follow the river bank to
another stile, cross and continue to a double stile. The path leads
away from the river to the right and uphill to another stile. Cross
the field to the next stile, then follow the wooden fence in the next

field to a stile into a lane.

Turn left and follow the lane down to the river. Turn left here, over the River Chew into the grounds of Byemills. Bear right, pass one stile on your right and then ahead are two metal gates, one for horseriders. Go through this and head uphill, following the right-hand hedge. At the top, the field narrows and becomes little more than a green lane, twisting to the left and then the right. Go through another horseriders' gate (Is there a technical term for these?).

On your left is the site of an old colliery, possibly the one called Rydon's or Riding's, though on the map the site is named Old Down. Rydon's started in 1808, but closed in about 1832 when it became flooded.

Follow the right-hand hedge to the road. As you approach the road, on your right you can see Stanton Drew church. To the right the white hexagonal building is an old toll house and between the two are the stone circles which Pevsner, in The Buildings of North Somerset and Bristol describes as 'the most important prehistoric monument in Somerset', dating from the Bronze Age. Recent research has discovered evidence of more circles and it is said that this site could have been as important as Stonehenge.

At the road turn right, go down hill for about fifty yards. On the left a track meets the road, and on the far side of the track is a stile into the field. Cross this field, heading towards the left-hand hedge. This takes you down into a little valley with a wooden footbridge - the old stone bridge which used to be here has obviously collapsed. Cross the bridge and walk towards the stile ahead. Cross and turn right up the hill. At the top you can see the stone circle to the right of the church. Descend the hill, bearing left, to the bottom left-hand corner of the field. There is a stile here, although it had been uprooted the last time I passed by. On the other side is a stream which you have to jump across. Now follow the hedge and stream on your left.

At the end of the field you can see a stile, but just before you reach it turn left and cross the stream again and another stile. Now turn right and follow the right-hand hedge, which borders the garden of a bungalow. Cross the next stile, turn left and follow the hedge. Cross the next stile, by the side of an oak tree, then head to yet another stile, this time to the right of a holly tree. Carry on in the same direction and, as you begin to descend the valley towards the stream, bear to the right, following the left-hand hedge. A stile in the corner takes you on to the road. Turn left, then after a few yards turn right, over a stile into a field. Ahead of you is the batch of Bromley colliery.

The path follows the left-hand hedge and the stream, over more stiles, up to the batch. Turn to the right in front of the batch for a few yards to a wooden footbridge. This takes you close up to the batch. Keep right, and make your way through the undergrowth, taking care not to get snagged by brambles. Where the batch ends there is a stile straight ahead.

(The 'official' route of the walk is to the left, up the side of the batch. As this is rather strenuous and might be a bit overgrown, you could, instead, cross the stile and follow the right-hand hedge to the metal gates at the end of the field. Do not go through the gateway, but turn left and follow the right-hand hedge to the stile and the road. Turn left and walk to the entrance to Kelston Sparkes Plant Hire. This is the site of Bromley colliery).

Turn left in front of the stile and follow the path up the side of the batch. Near the top there is a post with a footpath sign, pointing left to the top. On the right there is stile. Cross and follow the right-hand fence to a gate. Put your hand through the wire on the gate to pull back the catch and carry straight on, through the yard of Kelston Sparkes Plant Hire. This is the site of Bromley colliery.

Bromley Colliery was working by 1893, although it may have started earlier than this. Its peak time was in the 1930's when it was producing over 1,000 tons a week. By the time Pensford Colliery opened in 1910, Bromley had become part of Pensford and Bromley Collieries Ltd., and a tramway was built across the fields from Bromley so that coal could be taken directly to the BNSR. This tramway was built to a two-foot gauge, and was about a mile long. It was originally worked by a small steam locomotive, built by the Avonside Engine Company of Bristol and named 'Bromley No.1'.

Above and Top: Pensford Viaduct

Left: Pensford Colliery Engine House undergoing renovation.

Later, rope haulage was used. The costs involved in transporting the coal and the high cost of extracting it ensured that the pit did not last very long after nationalisation. It closed in 1957. It was the last pit in Somerset to use horses underground and at closure they were still being used apparently. Some of their names were Paul, Tiger, Wake and Temple.

As you leave the yard, turn left and walk to the A368. At the junction, on the left, there is a stile on top of the bank. Cross, turn right over another stile and head across the field towards the left-hand edge of the mound on top of which are farm buildings. Cross the stile in the hedge and carry on in the same direction across the next field. There is a stile, a footbridge and another stile. Walk up to another stile ahead, then aim towards the row of cottages which is end on to you. To the right of this row is a stile into the road. Turn left and then right. This takes you past the Carpenter's Arms. A little further on the road bends to the left. You soon come to the site of Pensford colliery, with several buildings still standing.

Pensford Colliery was started in 1909. Two shafts were sunk in 1910, but there were great problems, especially with water, and regular coal winding did not begin until 1917. The First world War caused financial difficulties and it was not until after 1939 that the mine began to make a regular profit for its owners.

It was the first pit in Somerset to have pithead baths installed in 1931. When nationalisation came, it was the second largest pit in the coalfield, but it was in great need of modernisation. The seams were difficult to work and modern machinery would not have been very effective. The mine finally stopped extracting coal in 1958.

The last building on the right was where the main winding engine was situated. At the end of 1998 it was being refurbished to make what the bricklayers said was going to be a 'mansion or a castle'! It will be interesting to see how this is developed. On the opposite side of the road were the baths. A little further on, the tramway from Bromley ran under the road.

As I said in the introduction to this walk, the path through the colliery is being improved and is much easier to follow than previously.

Beyond the last building there is a stile on the right in a layby. Cross it and walk straight towards the batch. There are some new wooden steps going down to another level. Turn left (north) and follow the mound of the batch down and round to the right until you are walking back in the opposite direction (south). You might be able to make out, on your left, the route of the incline which led down to the BNSR. At this point it appears that you are walking into a dead-end, but the path turns sharply to the left and begins to descend quite steeply, with the edge of the main part of the batch on your right.

This takes you to a concrete stile and you now turn left along the trackbed of the BNSR for a few yards. Climb up the other side and cross another concrete stile. To the right of the house below there is a gate, and to the right of that, by the stream, there is a stile which takes you on to a track. (Be warned that in wet weather this part of the field is very, very muddy).

The track takes you up on to the A37. You can now follow the road downhill to the petrol station, by the side of which is a lane that will take you peacefully back to the starting point. Or you can take the first road on the right down the hill, and walk down a much quieter road back to the centre of Pensford, past another pub, the George and Dragon.

2 Clutton and Greyfield Pits

Distance:	5.5 miles
Starting Point:	Railway Hotel, Station Road, Clutton
Map Reference:	625592

The first time I walked this route was on a drizzly day in November. I was impressed by the beautiful valley named Long Lands, very peaceful, with trees on either side, a fast-running stream following the path. The second time I walked this route Long Lands was just as beautiful in the winter sunshine, but the path was so difficult after days of rain that I thought at one point that I would have to turn back. One side of the valley had been turned into mud by pigs and I hardly had time to appreciate the beauty of the valley as I struggled to keep my footing. But to compensate for this, at one point in the walk, there was a spectacular view to the north where I could see the Cotswolds and the hills of the Forest of Dean above the towers of the old Severn Bridge.

This walk also brought home to me how much work had been done over the past 13 years by local rambling groups and county footpath officers. Every path was marked and one I had hoped to walk for the first edition of this book, but which was completely obliterated, had now been cleared, with new stiles and signposts.

Because of this, the route is easy to follow, though it can be difficult in wet weather.

In *The History and Antiquities of Somerset,* John Collinson, writing at the end of the eighteenth century, said of this area, 'The country abounds with excellent coals, the veins of which are generally covered with a stony stratum which the miners call Wark.' There has been a long history of mining around Clutton and the first recorded reference is 1597 when there was a dispute over a coal miner not filling in his disused coalpit, and between 1663 and 1671 thirty seven pits were sunk on the Earl of Warwick's estates. In the second

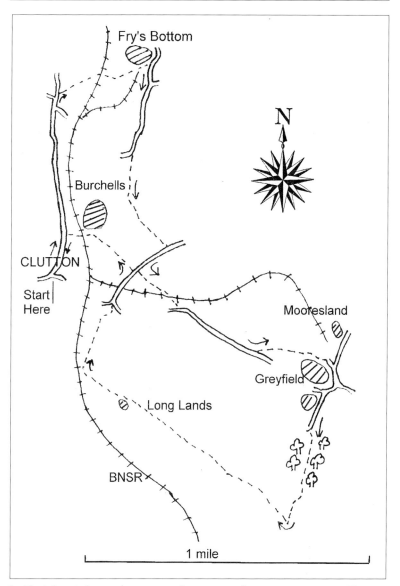

half of the eighteenth century there were three main pits on Clutton Hill, Clutton Upper Works, Engine Pit and Clutton Lower Works and old workings have been found in Greyfield Wood as well as other sites.

The walk starts in Clutton, along Station Road, in front of the Railway Hotel. Bear left to the side of the pub, along the Lower Bristol Road.

Almost immediately on the right was the approach road to Burchells pit. There was a drift mine here and also a shaft further to the north on the other side of the railway line which you will pass close to later on in the walk.

Further down the road on the right, you pass Burchell House and then Burchill Close. The entrance to the drift was up on your right.

As you pass the signs indicating the end of the 30 mph zone, on your right you might be able to see the ivy-covered chimney which stood on the site of the other part of Burchells pit. There is a tree-covered batch here. One of the shafts was close to the chimney and there was another behind the batch.

Burchells or Clutton Colliery began when it became obvious that nearby Greyfield pit was nearly exhausted. Work started in 1908 or 1909 to open an old shaft and to open a very shallow drift, following the seams. Fred Flower, in his *Somerset Coalmining Life*, suggests that the workings were so near to the surface that the miners were able to hear the trains running above them. Men and machinery were transferred here about 1911, but the pit did not last long. In 1920 there was a partial flooding and it closed in 1921.

Continue along the road for about half a mile. King Lane joins the road and shortly after there is a bungalow on the right. Beyond, opposite the entrance to Northend Farm, lying a few yards back from the road, there is a wooden gate on the right and a stile by the side of it. Cross the stile, then another one, into the field. Follow the left-hand fence down hill to another stile, cross over and continue down hill following the fence which is now on your right. This brings you to a metal stile which takes you to the trackbed of the BNSR. Turn left for a few yards, then right down the wooden steps to the stream. Cross the bridge and the stile beyond it. Climb up the hill into the field and head towards the white cottage beyond the hedge and road. On your left, as you ascend the hill, is the batch of Fry's

Bottom Colliery. Near the top of the climb you cross the route of a siding from the BNSR. To the left of the cottage is a gate and stile into the road.

At the road, turn left to look more closely at the batch, which is private property. The shaft was close to the road. The white cottage, Poacher's Pocket, was once part of the colliery, probably offices.

Fry's Bottom Colliery, like Greyfield, Burchells and Mooresland, was owned by the Earl of Warwick and at work by 1838. At first coal was wound in hudges – iron tubs or barrels – and a horse gin provided the power. Later a winding engine with a steam boiler provided the power. Probably in 1876, the siding from the BNSR was opened, but the pit closed permanently in 1893.

Walk a few yards further on to look at the lovely view towards the Cotswolds and the Forest of Dean.

Now turn round and follow the road uphill. Where the road forks, turn right. Along here, if you look to the north, you might be able to pick out the towers of the old Severn road bridge.

Where the road bends sharply to the right downhill, there is a stile on the left. Cross this stile and turn right. Cross the farm track and follow the right-hand hedge downhill. You can see again the batch of Burchells pit on your right.

At the bottom of the hill there is a stile in the hedge on your right. Cross it, turn left and follow the track. This leads you to farm buildings. Carry straight on, past the large barn on your right, until you reach the road - Clutton Hill.

Turn right and descend the hill until you come to the signs marking the start of the 30 mph zone. There is a stile on your left. Cross into a field, carry on to another stile, cross and make for the bottom left-hand corner of the field. Turn to the left, following the left-hand hedge to a stile which takes you up on to the trackbed of the railway which connected Greyfield Colliery to the BNSR at Clutton. After five yards there is path down the other side of the embankment, by some conifers, to a stile into a back garden. Turn left along the back of the gardens to a wooden fence. Follow the footpath sign to the right, along a garden path to the road at the back of the houses. Walk between the houses to reach the road at the front. Turn left and follow the hard track towards the batch of Greyfield colliery.

After about 500 yards, the track crosses a stream. On the left there is a stile. Cross into the field and follow the left-hand hedge. Another wooden stile takes you between a building on your right and what appears to be a builder's yard on your left. This yard was once the site of Greyfield brickworks and just beyond it was the entrance to a drift called Cuckoo drift. Beyond the yard, up the hill, was Mooresland colliery.

Greyfield Colliery, former engine house.

Greyfield began life in the 1830's and Mooresland in the 1840's. At some time they were connected so that all the coal from Mooresland was brought out at Greyfield via a drift called 'Cuckoo'. The shafts and many of the underground inclines were wound by a steam engine and, later, electric hauling machines were used. By 1859, after much modernisation, and with output at 60,000 tons, it was one of the most important mines in Somerset.

At one time there was no proper road access and so a tramroad was built to a coal depot on the Bath to High Littleton road. Soon after, a road was built. A siding was built to the BNSR at Clutton, about a mile away, opening probably in 1876. As the pit was higher than the sidings at Clutton, it seems likely that the full wagons ran by force of gravity to the station and the empty wagons were hauled by horses back to the pit. A few years later, small steam locomotives were used.

In 1904 Cuckoo drift was closed and the brick works closed in 1909. The same year there was a major flood and, although the pit was soon cleared of water, by the end of the year some men had been given their notice. In 1911 the whole colliery closed because Lord Warwick, the owner, refused to pay royalties to the owner of land under which the mine was being or about to be worked. This resulted in 152 men and boys being given the sack.

The path twists and turns and crosses two massive stiles made from iron girders. It then leads uphill into a housing estate – Gores Park. Turn right at the road.

As you leave the estate you come to a large stone house on your right. This was where the winding engine was housed. The road that leads uphill behind you, the Gug, at one time was a tramroad. At the top of the hill was a coal depot, and half way up the hill was the entrance to Mooresland pit. Although there has been much new building on the site of Greyfield, the batch is a prominent reminder of the industrial activity that once took place here.

Beyond the large stone house, called Greystones, above a low wall on the right were the shafts of the colliery. In 1986, the owner of the garden told me that when he bought the ground there was a toilet next to the concrete plug of one of the shafts. One day he threw a coin down and could hear it falling down the old shaft until it splashed into the water at the base. As the concrete plug was becoming unsafe he asked the NCB to fill it up.

Now follow the lane on your right. Another lane joins this one on the right, but do not turn down here. It is the lane you were following earlier and across it there was once a bridge which carried a track to a batch which was developed later. You can still see the abutments of the bridge.

Bear left down the stony track towards the woods. Opposite the house on the right is a lane on your left, which leads into Greyfield Wood, managed by the Woodland Trust. Follow the track through the woods. Where there is a kind of crossroads of tracks, carry straight on downhill until you come out into a field. Cross the field to a footbridge and cross the stream.

The route follows the path to the right. (If you have time, it is worth turning left to follow the stream to where it joins another and falls down a small waterfall. In winter it is quite spectacular, and the whole area is interesting to explore. At one time there was a shaft amongst the trees nearby).

Follow the path, with the stream on your right. This valley is Long Lands. There are one or two stiles along here, and when the woods on the other side of the valley come to an end the stream begins to bend away from the path. Cross the stile here into a field and follow the base of the hill on your left. At the end of this field there is an old metal gate, but the stile is some yards uphill to the left. Crossing this brings you into a fenced-off enclosure and you find yourself beneath a batch, presumably one of the old workings mentioned in the introduction to this walk. Follow the fence on your right to another stile which takes you back into a field.

Follow the left hand fence, heading towards the tower of Clutton church. This brings you to another stile and gate and there is a farm on your left. Continue towards the church tower, but before the next gate, which leads across the trackbed of the BNSR, turn right down the field, following the power lines. These lead you to a bridge over the stream. Turn right, follow the power lines, and to the right of the last bungalow there is a footpath which takes you to another footbridge and out on to the road - Maynard Terrace. To the left is Clutton Hill.

If you have done enough walking, you can turn left and follow the road back to the Railway Inn.

For a slightly longer walk, which takes you round the edge of the batch of Burchells pit, turn right up Clutton Hill, passing the bridge abutments of the siding which led from Greyfield to Clutton. Where the 30mph zone ends there is a stile on the left, opposite the stile *you crossed earlier. Cross the stile and when you come out into the field, bear left down hill towards the power line post. On your left, on the other side of the valley is the site of Clutton station.*

Cross the stile, head towards another stile and then towards the footpath signpost. Cross the stile here on your left, and the path leads down to a bridge over the stream. Follow the path uphill by the side of another stream, cross the railway trackbed, climb the stone steps and cross the next stile ahead, by the side of a house. Cross and walk alongside the house on your left. Before you cross the next stile, look back to the batch of Burchells pit. There is a better view of the chimney here, though it is so ivy-clad that it in summer it might not be obvious that it is a chimney.

The path takes you in front a bungalow and out into the road. Turn left to return to the Railway Inn.

3   Timsbury

Distance: 5 miles
Starting Point: Gus and Crook public house, Timsbury
Map Reference: 668586

This is an easy walk, except for a strenuous climb back into Timsbury at the end. There is also a stretch of road that needs care. The pits of Upper Conygre, Hayeswood, Mearns, Amesbury, Tyning, Old Grove and Withy Mills are passed, and there are glimpses of the Somerset Coal Canal and Camerton Branch Railway. You walk close by Rugbourne Farm where William Smith, the geologist, once lived.

The walk begins outside the Guss and Crook, a pub with an appropriate name for this area and it has a vivid and evocative sign hanging outside.

Walk up the road by the side of the pub and pass the church on your left. A little further on, there is a path on your right, just before the cemetery. Go through the squeeze style and follow the lane to the road. On your left can be seen the wooded batch of Upper Conygre Colliery. Turn left at the road and left again at the T-junction. The site of the colliery on your left is now used by a concrete block firm.

Upper Conygre Colliery opened in 1791. At first coal was disposed of by road, much of it to Bath. The hauliers would often stay overnight, sleeping in the colliery stables. Later, when Lower Conygre opened in 1858, some coal was sent by road to a wharf on the SCC, nearly a mile to the south. There was also an underground connection to Lower Conygre. Both pits closed in 1916 when the coalfaces came up against a major geological fault. Old photographs show the unusual chimney stack which was built of white stone. The top section was designed to look like part of the keep of a castle,

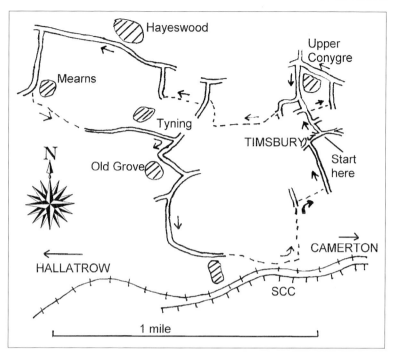

so that the view from nearby Timsbury Manor was not too spoilt.

At the crossroads turn left, back towards Timsbury and when you come to the new estate on the right, turn along the first road - Somerset Folly. This bends round to the left, then there is a small cul-de-sac on the right. This leads to a path in front of a row of bungalows, and this becomes a footpath with a hedge on both sides. At the end of the path a kissing gate takes you into a field. There is a fine view here. Ahead is the batch of Greyfield Colliery (see Walk 2), and below, to the left, is Rugbourne Farm.

Follow the wall and row of trees on your right. This route brings you to the road. Turn left and after 20 yards turn right along the track in front of a row of houses. Note the Paulton Foundry gateposts at the last house. The path goes straight on and comes out into another lane. Follow the lane round to the right, which leads to the main road. As you pass the field on your left you may be able to discern that the grass is a darker colour in places. Old Tyning pit was situated here at the top of the field. By the side of this lane a tramway led from Hayeswood, past New Tyning, at the bottom of the field, to the SCC at Paulton Basin.

When the lane reaches the road, turn left. This can be a busy road and there are one or two bends in this section, so take care. On your right you pass the site of Hayeswood Colliery, which is now occupied by Timsbury Village Workshops. You can see the pumping engine house and the batch.

Hayeswood Colliery opened about 1750 and closed in 1845 after a disastrous flood in which seven men and four boys were drowned. A newspaper report of 18th October 1845 noted that the men killed in February had at last been found. It was back at work in 1856, but closed for good in 1862.

Continue along the road for about 400 yards and turn down the next road on the left. Down the hill, the houses on the left occupy the site of Mearns pit.

Mearns Colliery was opened about 1783 and closed about 1817. William Smith surveyed it in 1792, probably the first that he surveyed, and said that the daily output averaged 20 tons produced by sixteen men and five or six boys.

Where the road bends to the right, continue down the lane straight ahead and cross the stile into the field. Note the small coal tips on the right. Straight ahead is Rugbourne Farm, once called Rugbourne House.

It was at Rugbourne House that William Smith (1769-1859), the 'Father of English Geology', lodged from 1792 to 1795. He called the house the 'Birthplace of Geology' and in his diary stated that he 'resided in a part of the large old manor house belonging to Lady Jones, called Rugburn. It was then occupied by a farmer who lodged and boarded me for half a guinea a week and kept my horse for half a crown a week.'

It was while he was here that he first recognised that different strata contain different fossils and realised that often a bed of rock could be identified partly by studying the fossils found within it. Many of the names still used to describe strata of the Jurassic System were first used by Smith.

William Smith came to Somerset in 1791, employed to survey an estate at Stowey. Next he was asked to make a survey for High Littleton Coal Co. In 1793 he was engaged by Rennie to help with surveying the SCC and in 1795 he became surveyor. Because of the researches he made at this time, he was able in 1801 to publish his 'General Map of Strata Found in England and Wales', the first geological map of its kind. While he was working on the SCC he often stayed at the Swan Inn, Dunkerton. In 1799 he seems to have been sacked. There may have been disagreement about the way he purchased a cottage at Tucking Mill, near Midford.

In 1932 the Bath Natural History Society and the Geological Society of London erected a plaque on what they thought was the house. However, according to a note in 'Geological Excursions in the Bristol District', edited by R.J.G.Savage (University of Bristol, 1977) the actual house owned by Smith is 100 metres to the east.

Another story about his sacking is that he underestimated the costs of the canal. However, he stayed in the area, setting up business with a partner in Bath as a land surveyor. In 1811 and 1812 he was called upon by the SCC management to deal with leakages in the canal bed.

Cross the stile on your left and descend the steps. On your left is the overgrown site of the colliery. One of the shafts was just on top of the rise. Follow the path, cross the stream and carry on to the buildings you can see ahead. This path was possibly a tramroad which connected with others which eventually led to Paulton Basin. The path brings you to a lane. The houses here once clustered round the Amesbury pit, the shaft of which was on the right. Note the old coal wagon in the garden of the first house on the right.

Amesbury pit or Allens pit was probably at work as early as 1701 and did not close until the early 1800's. There was probably another colliery further down the hill called Brombel or possibly Allens

Paddock Coal Works. There were many shafts in the area and it is virtually impossible to work out precise details about them.

Carry on along the lane. Past the houses, on the left, you can see the remains of the batch of Tyning colliery.

Old Tyning Colliery was situated at the top of this field, but there are no obvious signs now that it existed. It probably started in the 1760's, but closed about 1792 when New Tyning opened. The batch you can see is that of New Tyning, which apparently had a Newcomen type of steam pumping engine. The pit shut down in 1856, though it still pumped water for another pit further along the hillside – New Grove Colliery.

Continue along the lane until you reach the road.

This road is called Prior's Hill and up the hill, a few yards on the right, was once another small colliery. There is little information about Priors pit which seems to have been working in 1792.

Turn right down the hill. Where the road bends sharply to the left there was an entrance to Old Grove Colliery.

Old Grove Colliery started in 1766. In the mid-nineteenth century, the shafts were deepened, one of them reaching a depth of 1373 feet, so that for the first time a shaft passed through both the Radstock and Farrington series. By the 1860's, though, the pit was no longer prospering. Despite this, it continued working for a few more years. It was closed by 1878.

Follow the road to the T-junction. Turn right and where the road turns sharply to the right downhill, take the lane which forks to the left, signposted Withy Mills. You can easily see on your right the batch of Paulton Engine collieries, the site of Paulton Foundry and Paulton Basin. Follow the track as it bends to the left. This is the way to Withy Mills Colliery and the batch is clearly visible on the right.

94

Withy Mills Colliery was open by 1815. Coal was at first wound in hudges – iron tubs or barrels – but later cages were used. There was an incline on the east side of the batch down to a wharf on the SCC. The pit was closed by 1877.

The main buildings were on the left of the track which divides at this point. Bear right and follow the track through a gate towards the farm. Pass the farm on your right and, where you leave the farmyard, with a wooden notice on your right signposting 'House, Parking, Yard', there is a lane bearing up to the left. Follow this, passing an orchard on your left, until you come to stiles on your right and left. Cross the left one and climb up the hill.

At the top, bear to the right towards a stile into the housing estate. Go past the bungalows on your right, turn right between two rows of garages. Now follow the path alongside the right-hand fence, until you come to Mill Lane. Turn left and walk up to the main road in Timsbury. Turn right to return to the 'Guss and Crook'.

There are some interesting buildings in Timsbury and it is worth exploring the lane that leads up to the church and the High Street.

4 Lower Conygre, Paulton Basin and Radford

Distance:	3 miles
Starting point:	Junction of Weekesley Lane and Radford Hill, Radford
Map Reference:	673578

This is a short easy walk – just one or two hills – which passes the sites of Lower Conygre, Withy Mills, Paulton Engine and Radford collieries as well as the site of Paulton foundry. It also skirts Paulton Basin, the starting point of the northern arm of the Somerset Coal Canal, and for part of the route you will be walking along its towpath. It is easy to visualise what it might have looked like when it was in use, especially after wet weather when the canal fills up.

There is very little space for parking here, so take care. The best spot is probably at the bottom of Radford Hill, by the side of the old railway line, just before this road joins Weekesley Lane.

The walk starts on the old railway bridge at the bottom of Radford Hill where it meets Weekesley Lane. The railway was the Camerton branch which ran between Hallatrow and Limpley Stoke. Just to the west of the bridge there was a level crossing across the road to Timsbury. An incline from Lower Conygre colliery joined a siding here where coal was transferred to the railway. Also here was Radford Halt.

Walk up Weekesley Lane, signposted Tunley and Bath. When you come to a footpath sign on your right, just after the road flattens out for a while, cross the stile and follow the hedge back down hill for a few yards. In the wall here you should be able to make out the arch of a bridge. This is where another incline from Lower Conygre

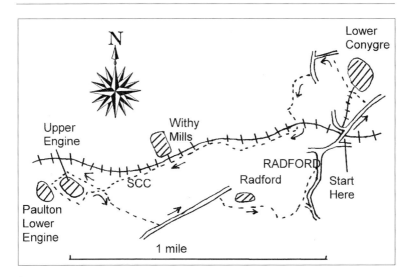

descended, to a wharf on the SCC. Return to the road, turn left and cross the stile on the other side. The path is between two wire fences and heads towards the edge of the batch. In this field, on the route of the incline, there were coke ovens, screens and a weighbridge. If you look at the batch you can, perhaps, make out the route of the incline which ran down to the canal.

Lower Conygre Colliery opened in 1858, although work started on it about 1847. There had been financial problems and difficulty installing the winding engine. A new underground connection was soon made with Upper Conygre in Timsbury and a tramway was used to transport coal to the SCC. In 1900 the incline to the GWR was opened. Much money was spent on exploration and modernisation in the first years of the 20th century, but there was little return. The pit was finally closed when it was flooded from the Withy Mills workings. It closed in 1916 at the same time as Upper Conygre.

The footpath goes through a tunnel under the other incline which ran down to the railway at Radford. At the other side, turn right and follow the path to a stile. Cross the stile and make your way to the top of the steep hill to a metal gate.

I have to confess that the last time I walked along these paths there was a bull at the top of this field looking down at me with what I imagined to be a stern expression on his face. I decided to take no chances and instead climbed up on to the incline and followed it to the top of the hill where it joined the lane. Although this is not a public right of way I felt this was a good example of discretion being the better part of valour etc. As it turned out, when I passed close to the bull in the safety of the lane, he looked rather peaceful, but perhaps this was an attempt to fool me.

Cross the gate into the lane and turn left to the road. Turn left downhill until you reach a signposted footpath on your right. Cross into the field, following the left-hand hedge until you reach another stile, quickly followed by another. Descend to the stream and bear left up the hill to the stile which takes you into Mill Lane. Follow it downhill. Ahead is the railway line. Cross the stile on to it, then cross another stile back into the lane. Ahead are some derelict buildings, presumably the mill. Close to this point was the site of the canal wharf which served Radford Colliery which was on the other side of this valley.

Cross the stile on the right on to the towpath of the canal.

There are another couple of stiles before the canal disappears for a while and you reach a lane leading to a farm on the right. Cross this track and continue in the same direction as before, following now the bed of the canal and crossing one or two stiles. On your right the tree-covered batch of Withy Mills Colliery appears. At one time there was a wharf for the colliery on the bank of the canal.

Withy Mills Colliery had opened by 1815 and had closed by 1877. When it was opened an incline was built to carry the coal down to the SCC.

Beyond Withy Mills the canal looks more like a canal again, with a towpath. When you reach the next stile you can see the basin of the canal beyond the bushes. This is Paulton Basin where the canal started on its meandering way to the Kennet and Avon Canal. Turn left here, then right, so that the river – Cam Brook – is on your left and the basin is on your right. There are the remains of various

98

*Above: Paulton Basin,
at the start of the
Somerset Coal Canal.*

*Left: Towpath of the
Somerset Coal Canal.*

bridges and arches here. These were part of the system of sidings wharves and overflow channels.

Cross the next stile and continue along the edge of the basin to the end. There is often plenty of water here, especially in winter. There were wharves on either side: on the other side tramroads ran down from Mearns and Hayeswood collieries (see Walk 3); on this side there were tramroads from Paulton Lower Engine, Paulton Upper Engine and also an incline from one of the pits in Paulton called Salisbury Colliery.

On the left is the batch of Paulton Lower Engine collieries.

At the end of the basin, look ahead to the metal fence across the field. Its style is very much that of Paulton Foundry which is only a few yards away.

Now turn left to the stile and bridge over the brook. This is the route of a tramway. You will notice that the batch is now a wildlife conservation area. Ahead is the sewage works which is on the site of Paulton Lower Engine. Turn left, following the path between the batch and the works until you come to a stile. Beyond was Paulton Upper Engine and beyond that was Paulton Foundry.

Paulton Engine Colliery is said to be the earliest pit in this part of the coalfield. It probably takes its name from the fact that it had a steam engine to pump water. It began work in the second half of the 18th century, perhaps as early as 1750, and it continued working until about 1870.

Paulton Brass and Iron Foundry was established in 1810. By 1839 it was in the hands of William Evans and Paulton Coal Company. It was probably working up to the 1890's and was the only major foundry in the North Somerset Coalfield. It made winding engines, pumping engines etc, as well as domestic items. It is still fairly easy to find the large cast-iron gateposts at the entrances to drives and fields. It probably closed about 1890, but then a new business was set up close to Lower Writhlington Colliery near to Radstock. Later it moved to Frome Hill, Radstock, but closed several years ago.

Turn left between the batch and the cottage, back towards the basin.
A bridge takes you over the brook. Turn right to another bridge
which takes you into a field, go straight across the field to a stile
and continue in the same direction to another stile which leads into
a lane. This crosses a track and leads to a drive to a house. This
takes you up to the road.

Turn left and, a little way along the road, notice the gate on the
left with its distinctive iron posts, undoubtedly made by Paulton
Foundry.

Shortly after the 'road narrows' sign, as the road begins to go
downhill, turn right up a lane, signposted 'Gingko House' (or is it
'Ginkgo House'?). Near the end of the drive turn left, following the
footpath sign to a stile. Cross in front of the stable to a couple more
stiles which take you into a field. On your left now is the batch of
Radford Colliery.

Radford Colliery was open by 1809. It was connected to the SCC by
a tramroad incline and is said to have closed in 1847.

Cross the field to a stile. Follow the right-hand fence up the hill.
There is yet another stile and the track now bends round to the
right, still going uphill. The track comes close to the stream on your
left. Go across it and over the stile. Now go uphill following a faintly
defined path to the power line post in the hedge. There is a stile here
which takes you on to tarmac drive. Immediately, turn left, off the
drive, down to a stone stile. Follow the right-hand fence down
towards a metal gate, by the side of which is a kissing gate on to the
road. Go on down the hill and turn right along the road to reach the
starting point in Radford.

5 Camerton and Dunkerton

Distance: 4 miles
Starting Point: Outside the Old Rectory, Camerton, on the road which leads to Camerton church.
Map Reference: 685573

This is an easy walk, apart from one steady climb, with good views across the Cam Brook valley. For part of the way the walk follows the route of the SCC and the Hallowtrow to Limpley Stoke railway. You will pass the collieries of Camerton and Dunkerton and also Camerton church where the Rev. J. Skinner was rector at the beginning of the nineteenth century. He wrote at length in his journal about the village and its inhabitants.

The Old Rectory in Camerton is half-way down the hill which leads from the Radstock-Bath road (the Fosseway) to Camerton. It is just along the road which is signposted 'To the church' and 'Church carpark'. The rectory was rebuilt in the 1840s and there is very little left of Skinner's original rectory.

From the rectory, walk to the road, Skinner's Hill, and keep to the right until you come to the entrance to Camerton Court. On the left of the drive is a small iron gate. Go through it and cross the grass to the kissing gate. Bear right and cross the field, passing to the right of the stone-built house. Beyond the house in the corner of the field there is another kissing gate. Go through it and now you can see the two batches of the Camerton pits, Old to the left and New to the right of it.

Beyond New pit you can see the road leading up the side of the valley to Timsbury. There was an incline from Camerton New to this road where there was a coal depot known as Meadgate.

About a mile along this road, to the north-east, where it joins the

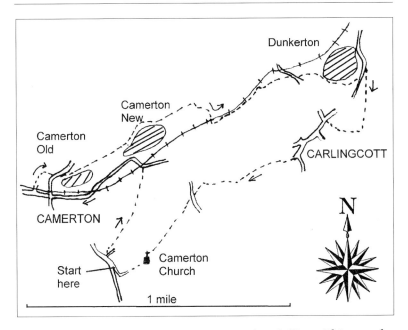

road from Carlingcott, was Priston or Tunley Colliery. This was the last deep mine to be opened in Somerset, work starting on it in 1914 and coal production beginning in 1915. It was hoped to build an aerial ropeway to Dunkerton, but this never materialised and coal was sent by road to the wharf at Radford and on to the Hallowtrow-Limpley Stoke line. The pit was sold to Sir Frank Beauchamp in 1923 and for a time it supplied Bath Gas Works. When this customer was lost, the mine closed down, in 1930.

Descend the hill, keeping parallel with the left-hand hedge, to the road. Turn left along the road. You can see one of the abutments of the old railway bridge on your right and, a few yards beyond, there are some cottages that were once part of the colliery as well as the wall which supported the colliery sidings. You can also see the embankment of the railway on the left. You cross over a railway bridge and the bungalows on the right are more or less on the site of Camerton station and its sidings.

When you reach the crossroads, go across into Durcott Lane. Take the second on the right, Collier Close. In front is the building

that was the Jolly Collier public house. Along the left-hand wall
there are some steps which take you on to the tow path of the old
SCC. Turn right here and return to the road. This was the site of
Camerton Old Colliery.

At one time, the road wound its way right through the centre of the colliery, with cottages and the smith's shop and its stables on your left, the pithead, across the road.

Camerton Old started producing coal in the 1780's and New Pit, which the walk passes later on, started at the beginning of the 19th century. The pits were connected underground and on the surface by tramways. Originally, the lease to work the coal was granted by the lord of the manor, James Stephens. When his daughter married Herbert Jarrett, the Jarretts gained control of the manor and the mines and the Jarrett family figure prominently in the history of the village in the 19th century. In 1911, the collieries were bought by Sir Frank Beauchamp. The Beauchamp family became one of the most powerful mine owners in Somerset, with mines at Farrington, Old Welton, Welton Hill, Norton Hill and Braysdown. The family also took over the Radstock collieries of the Waldegrave family.

The two Camerton collieries were both by the side of the SCC and when the GWR line was built a siding was laid to New Pit. There was also an incline up the northern slope of the valley to Meadgate Coal Depot.

In 1893, there was an explosion caused by coal dust igniting during shot firing, the first time that such an explosion had been recorded in Somerset.

Old Pit closed about 1898, but New Pit survived to be nationalised, although it closed soon after, in 1950.

Cross the road, go through the wooden gate, and you can see the
concrete plugs of the shafts of the colliery. Here there is a massive
statue of a miner. At one time this stood in the carpark of the Jolly
Collier, and, I believe, was originally constructed for the Festival of
Britain in 1951. There is also a plaque which gives information
about the village and its mines. Ahead is a heritage trail, which
takes you up and around the batch of the colliery and back.

Leave this site by crossing the stile by the information board. Turn right along the road, go through the gate signed 'Woodside', and you come on to a new estate of houses. Ahead is a lane leading towards the batch of Camerton New. On your right is the batch of Camerton Old and below it was the SCC. This lane was originally a narrow gauge tramway linking the two pits, and later converted into a road. When you arrive at Camerton New, you can, perhaps, discern the route of the incline up to Meadgate Coal Depot. There are several buildings here which were once part of the colliery.

Straight ahead is a wooden gate into the garden of the house on your left. You must go through this garden, so take care to keep to the path. To the right of the garage is a metal gate. This takes you into field and you now follow the right hand fence, along the edge of the batch. Cross the next stile, round the batch, then, as you start to follow a rough track downhill, keep over to the left-hand fence, so that you leave the batch behind you. In this field is a ridge which marks the route of the SCC. Do not go down this ridge but cross the stile on your left, which takes you round the back of a house and its garden. On the other side of the house drop down to the track.

The SCC swept away to the north at this point to follow the contour of the valley. Follow the track, cross the cattle grid, and just after the track cuts through the old railway embankment, turn left over a stile. Keep close to the left-hand fence, go up the rise and cross the stile on your left on to the trackbed. Turn right and follow the railway. On the right you can see Carlingcott Mill. Where the track becomes overgrown, turn right down some steps to the stile into the field. Carry on along the field to a stile which takes you to a lane.

Turn right down the lane, then just before the river, turn left along the path, with Cam Brook on your right and a small vineyard on your left. The path takes you across the river and on to the road. On your left is the batch of Dunkerton Colliery.

Dunkerton was a comparatively modern pit, with the first coal found in 1905. It soon became the largest colliery in the coalfield, but at the same time the methods used by the company gave it a bad reputation. The company cared more for its profits than the safety of its miners

Left: Statue of collier at Camerton Old Colliery.

Below: Cottages at Camerton New Colliery.

and it was this attitude that led to the riots that occurred during the 1908-9 strike. Down and Warrington give a graphic account of the events leading up to the riot and of the riot itself.

After the First World War the pit ran into financial difficulties and in 1925 it closed. Sir Frank Beauchamp took charge, but he was forced to admit defeat in 1927. There were many proposals for re-opening, right up to 1946, but none of them came to anything.

At the road, turn left. It is worth walking to the bridge over the river as it has an interesting metal notice attached to it. The entrance to Dunkerton pit is a few yards further on, but nothing can be seen of the site as it is now in private hands. Almost opposite the entrance, down a track, there is a bridge with narrow gauge railway track on it and handrails made of old railway lines.

Retrace your steps from the road bridge and on the left is an entrance to a farm. Next to it is a gate and a kissing gate. Go through, bear right and climb up the hill to another kissing gate. Continue in the same direction, but at the next, do not go through, but turn right and follow the left-hand hedge, through another gate, alongside a wooden fence to a wooden gate which leads you eventually round to the road.

Turn left into Carlingcott. At the tiny village green, bear left, then take the next lane on the right, where the road bends to the left.

This lane becomes a rough track. The track becomes very overgrown at one point and you might have to walk alongside it in the field. Just keep following the right-hand hedge as closely as you can. The track curves round to the right and then you come to a waymarked stile. Cross it into the field, follow the left-hand hedge to the brow of the hill. Ahead are Camerton Court and the church. The original court was much closer to the church, but was rebuilt in its present position in 1835.

Descend the hill, aiming for the church, to a stile into the road. On the other side, cross into the field and go up the valley, bearing to the left, towards the church. Follow the boundary of Camerton Court and then enter the churchyard.

Camerton church is worth exploring, with its very unusual carvings, its chapel of the Carew family and memorial to the Jarretts. Outside to the north of the tower is the grave of Anna Skinner, the wife of John Skinner.

John Skinner was born in 1772 near Bath and in 1800 became rector of Camerton. He married Anna in 1805 and they had five children. Unfortunately, only two survived him, and his wife died in 1812. He committed suicide in 1839 by shooting himself, in the woods above the church.

By reading his journals we gain a full picture of this exasperating man. He seems to have argued with everyone at one time or another, and yet he often realised how annoying he could be. He sympathised with those who were in trouble through no fault of their own, but openly criticised those who did not agree with his views. He found it difficult to compromise.

His journals create a fascinating picture of life at the beginning of the 19th century. Here are some short extracts from his journals to whet your appetite.

'1806 March 22. James Edwards, whose business it was to see the coal brought to land at The Old Pit, in reaching over too far to stay the basket which was coming up, fell to the bottom and was dashed to pieces. Horrid to say, his last word was an oath when he found himself going. He left a widow and four children at Cridlingcot.'

'1822 July 10. As there was a great shouting at the Coal Works, music playing, singing, etc., etc,. which I could hear from the Parsonage field, I imagined at first that the whole populace participated in the glad tidings which set the bells ringing; but Bacon informed me the Proprietors of the Works were present at the Bailiffs, and had distributed money, on account of the discovery of a fresh vein of coal, which promises to be very advantageous. This, I think, is very good news for the parish, as it regards the future prospect of so many who depend on the prosperity of the miners.'

'1824 August 22. I afterwards walked to Timsbury across the fields. In my way I stopped at Tyler's house at Daglan, and was destined to see the exhibition of the mangled face of the poor collier as he lay in his coffin. Surely the lower orders cannot have the same feelings as we have, otherwise they could take no delight in exposing what ought with the greatest care to be concealed, or in visiting what must convey sensations of horror rather than those of satisfaction.'

'1830 November 1. The evening was spent in looking over the coal fossils, and Shakespeare prints by Boydell.'

'1830 December 13. Soon after, I saw this mob proceeding to our pits. I then walked to Clan Down, having heard that there had been a mob of the colliers assembled there yesterday, and that the Riot Act was read. ... I saw all was quiet on the Down and the Steam Engine working as I approached the pit. I walked thither and found that the Radstock Rioters, for I can call them by no other name, had gone on to Paulton.'

When I talked to the rector of Camerton in 1986, he told me that, although Skinner had committed suicide and therefore should not have been buried in the churchyard, he believed that he was in the same grave as his wife.

Leave the churchyard by the main entrance and return to the starting point.

6 Paulton to Farrington Gurney

Distance: 5.5 miles
Starting Point: The Red Lion, Paulton
Map Reference: 651566

At one time there were many collieries in the Paulton area including Salisbury, Littlebrook, Crossways, Brittens Lower, Brittens New, Brewer's and Goosard, as well as the two which are covered in Walk 4 – Paulton Little Engine and Paulton Upper Engine. This walk passes three more - Paulton Ham, Paulton Hill and Simons Hill. The walk also looks at Old Mills, with its distinctive conical batch, Farrington and Marsh Lane.

There is a car park in the centre of Paulton on the Radford road, almost opposite the Red Lion.

From the Red Lion walk up the main road towards Midsomer Norton, past the war memorial on your right. When you reach the petrol station on the left, turn left along Ham Lane. On your left is a row of houses, Alexandra Terrace. Opposite the end of this row is an estate of bungalows. Turn right on to the estate, up Ham Grove. Follow the pavement to a large stone stile.

Squeeze through into the field, and follow the path uphill. As you approach the next stile, look back to the left where there are some garage buildings on the road. This is the site of Paulton Ham colliery.

Little is known about Paulton Ham except that it was working in the 1840s and had closed by 1864. There was a tramroad incline down to the canal at Paulton Basin which joined with other inclines from

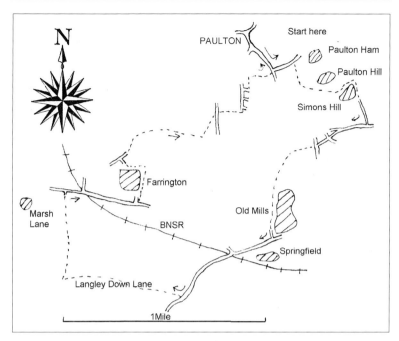

Paulton Hill and Simon Hill.

- *Cross the next stile on to a track. This, presumably, was the entrance to Paulton Hill colliery. Turn left, then cross the stile immediately on your right. Walk diagonally across the field towards the large batch ahead. As you do so, you will notice a small batch on your left in front of the house. This was the site of Paulton Hill.*

Once again, Paulton Hill was working in the 1840s, but had closed by 1864.

- *Head towards the top right-hand corner of this field where there is a stile. Turn right and then cross the stile on your left. The path follows the edge of the batch to the top of the field to another stile. Before you cross this stile, it is worth walking to the edge of the batch to see the view across Paulton to the Mendips. Below is the football ground and the batch makes a superb grandstand.*

111

This is the site of Simons Hill colliery. It was working in 1791 and closed about 1844.

> *Return to the stile, cross and walk up to the stile and hedge. Do not cross this stile, but turn right and follow the left-hand hedge. This takes you to a stile and a gate which takes you into a lane and this leads to the road from Paulton to Clandown. Turn right and continue to the main road. Opposite is the Bloomfield Care Centre. Walk into the grounds of the centre and follow the road to a stile. Ahead, a metal stile takes you into a field. Keep to the right, along the back of the bungalows, and walk to another stile. Turn left and head across the field towards the right-hand side of the batch of Old Mills. To the right of it are the DIY store and its offices, Great Mills.*
>
> *As you begin to descend the hill, make towards the two wooden power line posts and just beyond them are a stile and an iron gate. Cross the next field to a stile between the batch and the offices and follow the road to the main road.*
>
> *The wall on your left supported the lines which at one time carried coal to the screens on the other side of the road in Springfield colliery, and later waste from Springfield to the Old Mills batch. One of my early memories of the coalfield is seeing one of the small wagons reach the top of the batch and tip its contents, as I travelled from Bristol to Frome along the BNSR.*

Old Mills was started in the 1860's, the first coal leaving the colliery about 1864. Nearby, across the main road, was Springfield Colliery. This started a few years later and both were owned by the same partnership. One of the partners was William Evans, who also owned Paulton Foundry. The two collieries were connected by a tramway above ground, and eventually were connected underground. The Old Mills shaft was only used for ventilation and winding supplies after 1941, but at nationalisation the colliery took the name of Old Mills rather than Springfield.

New owners modernised the pit substantially in the 1930's, and the NCB continued doing so. The pit closed in 1966, partly, it is said, because there was a labour shortage and the men were needed in other local collieries.

Above: Batch of Old Mills Colliery;
Below: Miners Arms, Farrington Gurney.

113

Great Mills, the DIY chain, I believe, opened its first shop here with the name Old Mills, but changed its name a few years later, presumably because the new one sounded more impressive.

In 1986, the winding house of Springfield colliery was still standing as were the huge metal gateposts, obviously made at Paulton foundry. Also, the red brick bathhouse could be seen on the Great Mills side of the road.

Turn right along the main road – cross over on to the pavement – and take the next road on the left. This is Langley's Lane. Here you can see the bridge which crossed over the BNSR and on the right the trackbed is still plainly visible. This road crosses a stream and then passes an electricity sub-station on the right. If you look back to the batch of Old Mills, you can see to the right, the batch of Springfield and a long shed which possibly was once part of the colliery complex.

The road bends to the right and, on the right, there is a metal gate and wooden public bridleway sign. Follow the right-hand hedge to the gate which leads into the woods. This is Langley Down Lane which leads across the top of Hillier's Down for nearly three-quarters of a mile. To the north, across the main road to Farrington Gurney, you can see a new small industrial estate. This is the site of Farrington colliery. And along the valley to the west, you might be able to distinguish the small batch of Marsh Lane.

Where the lane widens out and there is a hedge across, there are stiles to right and left. Take the right hand stile into the field and descend the hill to a stile directly below. Now follow the left-hand hedge, cross the stream, and follow the path straight across the field. To the left, a couple of fields away, is the low batch of Marsh Lane pit.

Marsh Lane Colliery opened in the 1920's. About 20 miners who had lost their jobs in the area banded together to open their own pit. They raised coal from Church Field Colliery, a drift mine, for about a year, then moved to this site for safety reasons. The land was owned by the Duchy of Cornwall and no dues had to be paid until the pit was able to afford them. The mine was taken over at nationalisation by the NCB, but closed in 1949.

An old miner (82 years old in 1986) whom I met while walking along Langley Down Lane, told me that he was one of the original shareholders. He had been made redundant from Farrington pit and worked here until it closed in 1949. He remembers the Prince of Wales visiting the pit, and also the two lorries which were owned by the mine for delivering the coal. When the mine closed, he went to work at Old Mills. After that he worked in one or two other mines until he retired at the age of 62. When I met him, he had just climbed the steep hill without stopping and was obviously very fit, although he said that he had given up cycling two years before. He was carrying his home-made saw to collect wood. One of his achievements, of which he was very proud, was, many years ago, clearing Langley Down Lane so that it was passable again after many years of neglect. This is the lane which you have just walked, along the top of the hill.

Cross the stile into the road and proceed to the main road. Turn right and pass the Miners Arms. Note, at the side of the pub, the ticket office with its GWR sign. At one time, passengers who boarded the train at Farrington Halt bought their tickets here. The station itself was a few yards beyond the pub on the right and if you look on the opposite side of the road you can probably see the route of the BNSR, approaching the junction of the Paulton road with the Midsomer Norton to Farrington road. The line went under the junction. The station opened in 1927 and closed in 1959.

Carry on along the road towards Old Mills. On the left you can see the site of Farrington colliery. The industrial estate here is called Farrington Fields. On the right side of the entrance to the estate is a stile, with a red "path diverted" sign. Cross this stile and turn left, following the fence. In 1986, part of the electricity power-house was still standing, but now there is nothing left, although one of the houses amongst the cottages on the other side was once the colliery offices.

Farrington Colliery opened in the 1780's, but working was hampered by flooding and for a time it closed down. During the 19th century, ownership changed hands several times until the Beauchamp family took over in the 1880's. The pit was modernised and deepened and a siding was laid alongside the BNSR to a connection at Old Mills. It is possible that this siding was worked by horses for a time. Early in the 20th century, there was also an electricity generating station. During the 1921 miners' strike which affected most pits in Somerset, Beauchamp warned that the pit would close if the miners did not go back to work. The pit was closed.

At the back of the site turn left, following the fence to a stile. Cross a small field or paddock to another stile and then follow the track between the cottages. This leads to a road (Ruett Lane). Turn right along the track. The track twists and turns, gradually climbing towards the grass-covered reservoir. After a couple of stiles you come out into a field with the memorial to the men killed in this field when their gliders crashed on the way from Keevil, Wiltshire, to Arnhem in 1944.

Follow the right hand hedge, then bear left, crossing the field diagonally to the road. Cross straight over and follow the track across the recreation field which, according to a plaque on the side of one of the buildings, was bought for the community by Paulton miners.

On the other side of the field, you come to an estate. Turn left, through the squeeze stile into Plumtre Road. Near the bottom, turn right along Plumtre Close, by the swimming pool. Just before the entrance to the school, turn left down a lane.

If you continue down this lane you will eventually reach the war memorial in the centre of Paulton.

Alternatively, my preferred route, just before you reach the houses on your right, turn right through the playing field of the school. The path brings you to concrete steps which take you to a narrow walled lane and under a very low archway to the main road, opposite the petrol station. Turn left to reach the Red Lion, the starting point.

7 Radstock, Clandown, Welton and Midsomer Norton

Distance: 5.5 miles
Starting point: Centre of Radstock
Map Reference: 689550

This walk passes some of the Radstock and Midsomer Norton collieries which developed along both sides of the valley. The walk climbs north out of Radstock to Clandown and then follows the Fosse Way for a short distance. There are fine views across to the Mendips and particularly of Downside Abbey before the walk descends to the centre of Midsomer Norton and Norton Hill colliery.

The walk begins outside the Waldegrave Arms in the centre of Radstock.

The hotel is named after the Waldegrave family. They were Lords of the Manor of Radstock and came to own most of the pits here, including Old Pit, Middle Pit, Ludlows, Wellsway and Tyning. The sinking of the first shaft at Old Pit in the 18th century seems to have been pure speculation. Anstie, in his *Coalfields of Gloucestershire and Somerset* says: 'Discovery of coal at Radstock must be regarded more as an accident than anything else ... it is not probable that those who sunk the 'Old Pit' at Radstock had any clear notion of the geological structure of the Upper Series basin at that date.'

Undoubtedly, the most striking figure of the Waldegrave family was Lady Frances Waldegrave, daughter of a famous opera singer, who married into the family. She was married 4 times and lived a splendid life, rebuilding her London home, Strawberry Hill,

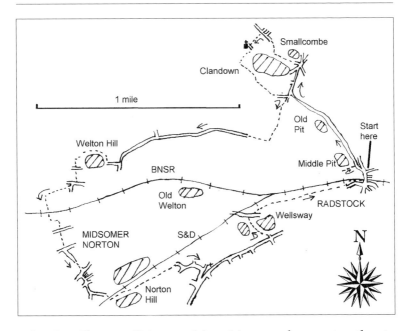

enlarging Chewton Priory and knocking two houses together in London so that she would have a big enough house for entertaining. Of course, the Radstock miners enabled her to do this.

Eventually, another famous local colliery owner – Sir Frank Beauchamp – gained possession of some of these pits.

The Radstock branch of the SCC started immediately to the south of the Waldegrave Arms and tramroads came from several collieries to the canal basin. The canal was eventually made into a tramway.

As you stand facing the Waldegrave Arms, turn right and go along the minor road to the left of Bath New Road. This is called Coombend. After passing the old chapel (now the Radstock Carpet Warehouse) turn up the lane on the left which leads through a car-breaker's yard. The large building on your right is the winding house of Middle Pit.

Middle Pit seems to have opened in 1779. At one time in its history it was the deepest mine in Somerset – 1,791 feet. By the end of the 19th century its coal was being taken out from nearby Ludlows pit, but the shaft was re-opened in 1906 with new winding gear. It closed in 1933.

Return to the road and continue along Coombend. On the left was a chimney, part of the colliery, and it was still standing when I first walked this way, but it has now been demolished.

Continue up the hill. The route of the tramroad which ran down from Clandown, Smallcombe and Old Pit collieries can just about be discerned on your left on the other side of the wall, opposite the fitness club. Old Pit was a little further up the road, mainly on the left. Two rows of cottages on the right have the name Old Pit Terrace.

Old Pit opened in 1763 and closed about 1854.

Ahead you can now see the batch of Clandown Colliery. At the road junction, turn right, uphill. This is the route of the Fosse Way. Pass the Lamb Inn on your left and at the T-junction turn immediately left, along the track at the back of the bungalows. In the field on the right was Smallcombe Colliery.

Smallcombe colliery started work in the last years of the 18th century. It was taken over by the Waldegrave family in 1847, but closed soon after, in the 1850's.

The track leads to the yard of Clandown Colliery. Just before you enter it, turn right up a tarmac footpath. When you reach the road, continue uphill until you reach the children's playground on your left. Turn left, go through the playground, past the swings etc, and cross the field to steps which lead down to the road in front of the church. Turn left, until you almost enter the old colliery yard.

Work started on sinking the shaft of Clandown colliery in the first years of the nineteenth century, but unfortunately a spot was chosen which lay along the line of the fault that runs through the area. By 1809, after going down 720 feet, it seemed that no coal was ever going to be found and work stopped. More money was raised and

Above: Middle Pit Engine House.

Left: Wellsway Colliery

Above: Five Arches: Somerset & Dorset crossing the Bristol & North Somerset Railway between Radstock and Midsomer Norton.

Below: Trackbed of Somerset & Dorset at Norton Hill Colliery.

work restarted. At last, in 1811, when the shaft reached 1,200 feet, coal was found. The pit was then worked until 1929, the last owner being Sir Frank Beauchamp.

Turn right down the lane which leads to a stile and into the field which borders the colliery. Cross another stile and turn left. Head towards the remains of a stone wall which is to the right of a bungalow. There is a stile here on the edge of the valley. Cross and bear left towards the bottom corner of the field where there is a wooden gate in front of a row of houses. The path leads under an arch into the road.

Go along the road, past the chapel converted into apartments, then turn right downhill. Keep to the right and follow the signposted byway over the stream. (The road which led to the left was the colliery tramroad to the SCC).

You are now back on the Fosse Way. It is a steep climb and it can be difficult in wet weather when the stones are slippery. At the top the track feels even more like a Roman road as it stands above the hedges on either side. Turn along the next lane on the right. This is Fosse Lane. After some distance, having passed two houses on the right, there is a gate on the left. From here look across the valley towards Midsomer Norton. Below you is the route of the BNSR and beyond is the route of the S & D climbing past Norton Hill Colliery towards the Mendips. Just the other side of the BNSR, where the industrial estate has been built is the site of Old Welton Colliery.

Old Welton colliery opened about 1783 and apparently prospered until the 1850's. It changed hands in the 1870's and William Beauchamp, the father of Frank, became one of the partners. A line was laid in the 1880's to the BNSR to replace the SCC tramroad, but the pit closed in 1896. However, Sir Frank Beauchamp took control of it in 1927 so that he could use one of the shafts as a ventilation and escape shaft for Norton Hill colliery.

The lane joins a road which soon begins to descend a hill. There is a bench on the left hand side of the road on the grass verge. Ahead you can see the batch of Welton Hill Colliery. When you reach the estate on your right, turn right along Green Tree Road. At the end of the road there is a footpath on your right between the drive up to number 12 and the house beyond. Turn up here and cross the metal stile into a field. The path follows the base of the batch. On the far side of the field, you skirt round the garden of a house to reach another stile on your left. In the garden were three shafts close to the footpath, and you may still be able to see the concrete plug of one of them. The main colliery buildings were clustered around these, and some of them in a derelict state can still be made out.

Welton Hill colliery was producing coal in 1815 and seems to have been a profitable pit. Up to 1880 there was a tramroad connection with the SCC at Radstock, but in 1880 a siding was opened to the BNSR, close to Midsomer and Welton station. Despite some modernisation in the 1860's, the pit was becoming unprofitable and eventually it was taken over by William Beauchamp in 1889. It closed in 1896.

Cross the stile and at the lane turn right, through what was the colliery yard. Cross over the road and continue down the track which follows the route of the tramway to the BNSR. At the main road there was once a bridge to carry the tramway. Turn right here and then left down Long Barnaby on to a new housing estate. Turn right along Barnaby Close, which leads to a footpath between the houses. Eventually this joins another path, so turn left down to where it crosses the BNSR. Carry on, cross the river, which has been given the name Wellow Brook, and turn left. At the end of the wall turn right. The route takes you across a road and alongside the football ground.

Cross the main road into North Way which leads to a lane down into the centre of Midsomer Norton. Turn right, then left up South Road. Continue uphill with the row of cottages on your left until the road forks. The old gas works building is on your right. Bear left up towards the batch of Norton Hill colliery.

Norton Hill colliery is often referred to as Beauchamp's Goldmine.

It started work probably in the 1840's and was bought by Frank and Louis Beauchamp in the 1890's, some time after it had closed. But then a new siding was laid to the S & D and a new shaft was sunk. When it re-opened it was the largest colliery in Somerset.

In 1908, there was an explosion in the pit caused by coal dust being ignited by flashes from shot-firing. Ten miners, including young boys were killed.

In the 1930's it was the largest producer in the area. Its average annual profit in the ten years up to 1946 was £50,000. At nationalisation there were big modernisation plans. Over £500,000 was spent and the number of men employed was to be increased to 800. Ten years later more modernisation was started, but a profit could not be made until a new, efficient conveyor belt was installed. Despite all this investment the pit was closed in 1966 because of geological difficulties and a manpower shortage.

The path takes you past the abutments which once supported the S & D bridge. The path bends to the left. There is another abutment near the top where a bridge crossed over the S & D, carrying a line to the batch from the main colliery buildings and shafts.

At the top the path divides. Take the left hand, lower path. When you reach the housing estate turn right and follow Ruskin Road to the Wells Road. Turn left towards Radstock. Follow the busy main road for half-a-mile. Opposite Maple Road turn left along a lane signposted Fosseway Cottages. On the right can be seen the engine house of Wellsway Colliery.

Wellsway Colliery opened in the 1830's. From 1897 coal was taken underground to Ludlows pit in the centre of Radstock to be brought to the surface. It is not surprising, because of this long and difficult journey, that the pit started to lose money. It closed in 1920.

Follow the lane as it twists and turns down the hillside between two batches. (Take care if the ground is wet as it can get slippery, especially as you come out on to the road at the bottom). Notice the miners' cottages at the bottom of the hill. When you reach the road note where the S&D once crossed over the road.

Turn right, cross the road and follow the path on your left, between fences, which crosses the river. This brings you to the viaduct which carried the S&D over the BNSR. The railway lines have now been developed into a linear park and it is a pleasant walk back into Radstock.

As you approach Radstock there are a couple of bridges leading under the S&D on your left. These show the routes of old tramroads.

8 Radstock, Braysdown, Foxcote and Writhlington

Distance: 5.5 miles
Starting point: Centre of Radstock
Map Reference: 689550

A straightforward walk, with two or three steep climbs. It passes several collieries to the east of Radstock. There are good views of Wellow Brook, of Radstock itself and of the route of the Somerest and Dorset Railway.

> *The walk starts from the centre of Radstock, by the large wheel close*
> *to the market hall. This is part of the winding gear of Kilmersdon or*
> *Haydon colliery. Turn right up the Bath Old Road, opposite the*
> *Waldegrave Arms. The first road on the right is Waldegrave Terrace*
> *and, although this is not part of the route, you might like to look at*
> *this row of typical miners' cottages built by the Waldegraves. Carry*
> *on up the hill into Woodborough Road and turn right along*
> *Shaftesbury Terrace.*

The cottages in Shaftesbury Terrace and Waldegrave Terrace are like the ones Janet Tanner describes in her novel *The Black Mountains* which is set in Hillsbridge, a small town very similar to Radstock. She describes the town as being 'set in a valley bowl, there was no way out of it except up a hill.' As one of her characters looks down from her house in the centre of the town, the narrator says: 'From here it was plain that the town had been built around the railway lines that would carry the coal out of the valley. They ran arrow-straight through the untidy jumble of dust-blackened buildings.'

The Black Mountains is a fascinating book, much of it based on

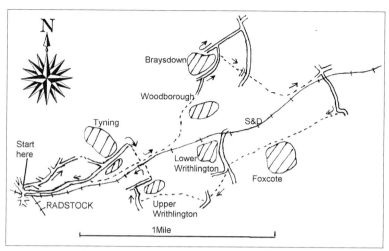

stories the author heard from her father and other colliers. Although it is a work of fiction, it creates a vivid picture of life at the turn of the century.

Shaftesbury Terrace leads into a lane which passes in front of the Tyning Inn. As the lane bends to the right, the batch of Tyning pit is on your left. You come into Stoneable road which brings you to the top of Tyning Hill. Turn left. The road runs between two batches which have been landscaped by the National Coal Board. On the right were many of the buildings of Tyning Colliery. At one time a railway incline led up to Tyning as well as a separate tramway to convey waste, mainly from Ludlows pit in the centre of Radstock, to the tip on your left.

Tyning Colliery began working in the 1830's and was taken over by the Waldegrave family in 1847. In 1873, the pumping of water from several nearby pits was centralised at Tyning. It was flooded seriously at least twice and when it closed in 1909 the pumps carried on working. It closed completely in 1922, although both Ludlows and Middle Pit continued to tip waste here until they too closed.

Now turn right down the lane past the two rows of miners' cottages, Lower Whitelands or Tynings. Note that there are few windows on

*the northern side, and also the long gardens which, I have been
assured, the miners used to take great pride in.*

*At the bottom of the lane, turn left along the track bed of the S &
D. Just beyond the last garden there is a footpath on the left, through
a gap in the hedge, just before the power line post. Turn immediately
right and follow the path to a stile into a field. Follow the path up
the hill, to the left of the oak tree in the middle of the field. Continue
up the hill towards the farmhouse, which is visible beyond a metal
gate.*

*Behind you is the tree-covered batch of Writhlington pit, which
has been worked to remove coal and shale.*

*Go through the gateway and follow the track through the
farmyard up the hill. On the right can be seen, first Woodborough
Cottages, then the batch of Woodborough Coolliery.*

Little is known of Woodborough Colliery. It probably closed in the
1840's.

*The track now approaches the batch of Braysdown Colliery. As the
track bears to the right there is a noticeable gap in the trees. Through
here was an incline which led down to sidings on the S & D.
Continue along the track until you come to a T-junction. Turn left
and walk along to the unusual entrance of Braysdown Colliery.*

Braysdown began working in the 1840's. The incline, built in the
1850's, originally carried coal to the SCC tramroad, but was replaced
in the 1870's by a new incline which connected to the S & D. In 1899,
Frank Beauchamp took control and it continued up till 1959.

*Return to the T-junction. Turn right, back along the track to
Woodborough, towards the batch of Braysdown. Before you reach
the batch, there is a stile on your left with the path clearly signed.
Cross it and make your way diagonally left across the field, well to
the left of the power line post and the bank which hides some
agricultural buildings.*

*If the day is clear, you can see ahead of you a row of buildings on
the horizon. This is Turner's Terrace, close to the village of Faulkland.*

At one time there was a tall tower at the left end of the terrace, called Turner's Tower, and close to it, to the west (right) a coal depot to which coal was sent by incline from Foxcote Colliery. According to the poet Edward Thomas, who cycled along the road just before the outbreak of World War One, a gentleman farmer named Turner built the tower 'as a rival to Lord Hylton's tower which we could see on our left at a wooded hilltop near Ammerdown House. Originally, it measured two hundred and thirty feet in height ... in course of time more than half fell down. The long hall at the bottom became a clubroom, where miners used to drink more than other people thought good for them. Finally Lord Hylton bought it: the club ceased.' At the time Edward Thomas passed by a hundred feet still survived of it, but now it has gone completely, although as you drive along the road you can just discern where it might have stood.

On the far side of the field is a plantation of new trees. Go through it to reach a black gravelled track which leads to the agricultural buildings. In the hedge is a stile, close to an ash tree, which leads to Braysdown Lane. Opposite is a gate and a way-marked stile. Cross the stile and walk down the hill. At the bottom of the hill is a gate in a dip. Climb over or squeeze under the gate if it is locked and follow the cattle track, bearing left, towards the farm buildings. Just below you, on a level with the farm buildings which are alongside the track of the S & D, must be the site of Shoscombe Colliery.

Shoscombe was begun in about 1828. It probably had a short siding to the SCC tramroad. It closed before 1860 and disappeared when the S & D was built across it.

Just before you reach the farm track, there is a stile on the left which leads to another one. This brings you out on to a farm track which once was the track of the S & D. Continue in the same direction, following the track to the road. You will notice that the railway swung off to the right here.

Turn right down the hill and past the abutments of the railway bridge. This is Shoscombe Vale. Follow the road, past the Foxcote Mill on your left, and up the hill.

Above: Lower Whitelands with the batches of Braysdown and Woodborough in background.

Left: Braysdown Colliery

At the top of the hill there is a stile straight ahead, to the left side of the entrance to a house. Cross it and follow the path to the right. This leads into a field. Follow the fence to the left and then cross another stile, descending the hill. Follow the hedge on your right until, just as you start to ascend, there is a stile on your right. Carry on in the same direction to another stile which takes you into the woods. The path is not always very clear or easy to follow here, so keep more or less to the right hand fence, with the batch of Foxcote Colliery on your left. You soon have to rise up to a level section. You should notice the track of the incline which descended from the main colliery buildings of Foxcote above you.

Foxcote, locally pronounced 'Fosscut', probably opened in 1859, but it was not very successful. Coal was taken by tramway either to Lower Writhlington colliery or to the coal depot near Turner's Tower . It managed to continue working until 1931.

You might notice some brickwork in the ground here. There was an engine shed here. Follow the track of the tramway until the woods end and cross a stile on your left into the field. Make your way along the bottom of the hill towards an entrance about 30 yards up the hill. Cross the fence on to the track which leads to the road. At one time there was a row of miners' cottages here.

At the road turn right to view the site of Lower Writhlington Colliery. You cross the route of the tramway and on your left you might see some of the tracks still in situ. During the writing of the first edition of this book the batch was still being worked and there were several buildings still standing. There is nothing left here now except a view through the trees on the left of the bridge over the stream which carried the railway lines to the S & D sidings. A little further on there still stands the bridge which carried the main line. On the right, the house stands on the site of various colliery buildings.

The shafts of Lower Writhlington were sunk in 1829. At one time, coal was transported by SCC tramroad to the GWR at Radstock, but in 1868 coal began to be taken by the S & D which had followed the route of the tramroad towards Midford. After nationalisation, there was some modernisation, although the men still had to go to Ludlows pit for their baths. The steam winding engine was the last to be used regularly in Somerset and was replaced in 1966 by an electric engine. It was one of the last to close, in 1973.

Turn back up the hill and take the right hand fork in the road. After a few yards, cross the iron stile on the left. Note the letters on the posts – WPC – which presumably stand for Writhlington Parish Council. The ironwork bears all the hall marks of the Paulton iron foundry. Take the path up the hill, which bears to the right under the power line. Follow the wall of the house on your left to the road. A few yards up the hill there is a gate on the right. Go through and head westwards along the top of the ridge, below the new houses, then drop down to the right hand fence towards the corner of the field. Cross the metal stile on your right. Below you is the incline which led from Upper Writhlington to one of the coal depots on the Frome Road, and on along to the GWR line south-east of Radstock.

Turn left and follow the path to the lane. Below you, on the right you can glimpse a house which stands on the site of Upper Writhlington Colliery yard. Further on, the house on the right is thought to be the colliery manager's house.

Upper Writhlington was ready to start working in 1805. It closed in 1898.

Turn right down the lane past the front entrance of the house, then bear left. At the bottom of the hill, turn right along the lane with the batch on your right. Turn left across the river, with the sewage works on your right and BOCM Paul's Radstock Mill on your left. It is interesting to compare the old mill at Shoscombe Vale with the new version.

The path brings you out on to the S & D again, below Whitelands. Turn left along the footpath towards Radstock. The path eventually bends right to the road. Once there was a bridge over the path which carried the incline from Ludlows to the batch and some iron rails can be seen acting as railings above you. At the road, turn left and return along it to the start.

9 Radstock to Kilmersdon

Distance: 5+ miles
Starting point: Centre of Radstock
Map Reference: 689550

The walk starts in the centre of Radstock, close to the new museum in the old market hall. There is a climb up Frome Hill before it descends to the peace and quiet of the valley which leads to Kilmersdon. On the return to Radstock, the walk passes the site of Kilmersdon or Haydon colliery before descending to another peaceful valley which leads to the centre of Radstock.

Before you start the walk, note the large wheel by the market hall. This is part of the winding gear from Kilmersdon colliery. At one time the S & D crossed the main road here and the station was where the car park is now. To the south, where the double mini-roundabouts are, was the level crossing where the GWR crossed the road. You can imagine the problems caused when one or two of the sets of gates were closed for trains.

Turn east along the Frome Road. On the right was the BNSR station. One of the platforms is still there in the undergrowth, but the railway lines have now been removed. As the road bends to the right and then to the left you pass on the left some of the buildings of the Ludlows colliery. The site now belongs to Charlton's World of Wood. Behind it the small wooded hill is the remains of a small batch. On the right, as the road crosses the stream, you can see another small bridge. In the 19th century this carried a tramroad which took coal to the BNSR. At the entrance to the colliery on the right you can still see railway lines embedded in the road. There was a standard gauge level crossing here, and also at one time there was a narrow gauge track that went under the road. Several colliery buildings are still standing. Particularly noticeable is the red brick building which housed the baths.

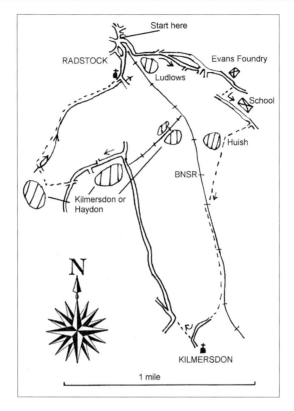

Ludlows colliery, pronounced locally 'Ludluss', was ready to raise coal about 1784. In 1897 it was connected underground to Wellsway colliery, three-quarters of a mile to the west, so that all coal was brought to the surface here. There was also a connection to Braysdown, and when Ludlows closed, its shaft remained as an upcast for Braysdown pit, ie air was driven up the shaft for ventilation purposes. Although there was a small batch at Ludlows, it was soon necessary to tip elsewhere and an incline was built to Tyning pit. At the time of nationalisation it was realised that there were only a few years' reserves of coal left and it closed in 1954.

- *On the right up the hill is Frome Old Road. Walk up here. There is*
- *a good view across the valley of the rows of miners' cottages, as well*
- *as the batch of Tyning. Continue up the hill until you reach the old*

offices of the Somerset Miners' Association which still has its iron balcony on the side. It has now been converted into dwellings. Turn left, back to the main road and continue up the hill. After 100 yards there is a new estate. The building on the upper side of Maple Rise was once part of Evans Foundry.

Originally, this was Frome Hill Coal Depot. It was built because of the difficulty of transporting coal up the hill by horse and cart. A tramroad, powered by a stationary steam engine, brought coal up the hill from Ludlows pit. The depot opened in 1868 and closed in 1926, but in the 1940's Evans foundry, which had already moved from Paulton in the 19th century to a site near Lower Writhlington colliery, moved to this site. This one building remains now converted into a dwelling.

Continue up the hill, with its miners' cottages on both sides. At the top of the hill on the left is Hanover Court. This is the site of another coal depot.

About 1868, a narrow gauge tramway was laid connecting Foxcote and Upper Writhlington collieries to the GWR line, close to the Kilmersdon incline. A landsale depot was also built here at the top of the hill.

Opposite Hanover Court, on the other side of Frome Road, is a lane. This is the route of the tramroad which led to the BNSR. Follow this lane, with the school grounds on your left, until you come to Mells Lane. The tramroad went across the road and down to the railway. At one time it was possible to follow the route for a few yards, but when I last walked here it was completely overgrown.

Turn left along the road. If you look over the hedge on your right you should be able to see one of the batches of Kilmersdon colliery, and perhaps a gap in the trees where there was also an incline to the railway. Further on is the community of Haydon. To the left is the batch of Huish colliery. After a few hundred yards, turn right along a private road leading to Huish House. This was also the road to Huish colliery.

Coal was first brought to the surface at Huish in the 1820's. In 1855, the incline was laid to the GWR line. Huish closed in 1912.

As you approach the site of the colliery you pass on your right the weighbridge office, still standing, just. On the left, the offices have been converted into private dwellings. Follow the track across the cattle grid. The pithead and shaft with engine house and boiler were located here and an incline ran down to the railway.

Follow the track down to the left. You can now see the rails of the railway in the valley.

As you approach Huish House with its two kissing gates (why two?), which have all the hallmarks of being made at Evans' foundry, cross the stile to the right. Head on down the field in the same direction, with Kilmersdon church in the distance, to the kissing gate close to the railway bridge. Go under the bridge to another kissing gate, turn left and walk along the valley between the railway and the stream. After you have crossed a stile and a little wooden bridge, close to the embankment, the path bends away to the right to meet a lane close to the sewage works. Turn right towards the village of Kilmersdon. Where the lane bends to the left into the centre of the village, turn right up a path which leads to the village school.

Before taking this path you might wish to look around the village with its church of St Peter and St Paul and the Joliffe Arms. At the top of the hill you are about to ascend, there is a well and a school. This was the scene for the nursery rhyme of Jack and Jill. They were a man and wife, not children. The cottage where they landed after their fall is still called Tumbler's Bottom. The local name of Gilson is said to derive from 'Jill's son'.

Notice at the top of the hill that there is a well in the school grounds! Turn right along the road to Haydon. There are good views from the top of Haydon Hill. To the south-west is Ammerdown column, to the south the tower of the church at Leigh upon Mendip, close to the tower at Cranmore, and to the south-east is the tower of Downside Abbey. Ahead is a newer tower, that of Cellnet.

As the road descends towards Haydon, you can see the site of

Above: Ludlows Colliery.

Below: Former bath house at Ludlows Colliery.

▌ *Kilmersdon colliery on your left, which is now an industrial estate.*

The land here was owned by Lord Hylton of Ammerdown, who offered the lease to mine coal to the owners of the Writhlington group of collieries. After four difficult years spent in sinking the shaft, the first coal was sold in 1878. From the beginning, there was a standard-gauge railway and incline to the GWR. At the turn of the 20th century the shafts were deepened to cut more seams. In 1928, the first conveyor at the coal face was installed and ten years later there were four working. At that time, just before the Second World War, the pit was producing about 70,000 tons a year.

Although compared to some other mines, there was not a great deal of investment in Kilmersdon or Haydon, it made a profit in 1958 and continued to do so until 1966. Steam-winding equipment was replaced by electric winders in 1963 and 1965, and in 1966 battery locomotives from Norton Hill were brought here and used underground. Although other modern equipment, including coal-cutting machines and trunk conveyor belts, was installed, the pit closed in 1973.

Opposite the entrance to the trading estate there is a lane which follows the route of the railway which led to the incline. Along here you can still see wooden railway sleepers in the ground. The track opens out and you can see the route of the incline. Mike Vincent's book, 'Through countryside and Coalfield', has some marvellous photographs of the incline and a detailed description of how it was worked.

When you reach the T-junction, turn left into Haydon. Opposite the Post Office there is a lane. Turn right along what was once the trackbed of the railway which led to the main Kilmersdon batch. Go past the Haydon Que and Social Club, over the stile. The large batch has now been flattened and landscaped. Follow the route down to the right into the valley. The path leads up to a housing estate. Just before you reach the top, turn right along the side of the valley. The path heads back towards Radstock and descends towards the stream. Follow this stream, on its left bank, until you reach the lane by the side of Saint Nicholas's church. Turn left along the road to the centre of Radstock.

10 Chilcompton to the Nettlebridge Valley

Distance: 5.5 miles
Starting Point: Junction of Abbey Road and Rock Road on the south side of Chilcompton
Map Reference: 648509

This is a lovely country walk, though there are some stretches of road walking. The start was problematical when I was planning it because the path I wished to use was difficult to follow. I think this was the only path I ever came across that was almost impassable. So I have changed the walk slightly, though I have also given instructions for the difficult bit if anyone feels like a challenge.

The walk begins close to Downside Abbey and soon drops down into the quiet, beautiful Nettlebridge Valley which in these upper reaches has a magic of its own. In his 'Old Mendip' Robin Atthill devotes a whole chapter to this valley, with the title 'The River without a Name'. The river's source is Emborough Pool, but it soon disappears underground and does not surface again for half a mile. On this walk you pass by the point where it resurfaces, close to Blacker's Hill Camp. At one time there were cottages here and you can still see some ruined walls, as well as the remains of watercress beds. Robin Atthilll asks why this little community disappeared. 'There were still quarries and coal-pits at work close at hand; there was still good land to till. Yet the fact remains that less than a hundred years ago there were between half a dozen and a dozen inhabited houses in the valley, served by decent lanes.'

First, the straightforward walk which passes Downside Abbey. The 'challenging' route is given below in brackets.

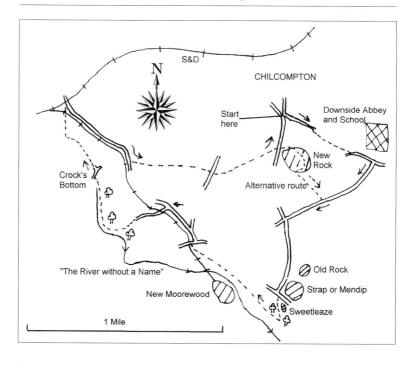

Go along *Abbey Road*, until you come to the metal gates across the road. To the right is a bridleway which takes you alongside the grounds of Downside School. On your right you can see the tree-covered batch of New Rock Colliery. You can see the layout of the site more easily at the end of the walk.

Probably the best account of the history of the mines in this area is in David J. Strawbridge's astonishingly detailed book *Meandering Through Chilcompton*. Not only does the book contain personal reminiscences, but it is packed with details about the mines and indeed the rest of the village. He recalls how his father told him 'how he was a young miner once, but left abruptly when his turn came to wear the guss and crook.' His grandfather was a miner for 52 years and was a local miners' representative.

New Rock colliery probably started working in 1819. In 1911 it was arranged to have a private siding laid at Chilcompton Station. It was also hoped to build an overhead ropeway from the colliery to the station, but this never came about. During the 1920's it was acquired by the Beauchamp family and an underground branch was driven to Moorewood Pit. Unfortunately Moorewood closed in 1932.

In 1947 the NCB made major improvements and in the fifties there was a grand plan to connect New Rock to Strap Colliery to the south. The reason for this apparently was that Strap had a larger shaft and coal would be brought out more easily here. By 1961, New Rock was employing 220 men and the coal was being transported by road to Portishead power station. When these two pits started working together in 1964, it was thought that there would be enough coal for 33 years' production. According to David Strawbridge, 'many chalets were erected adjacent to New Rock on the north side to house mostly miners and their families from Durham who had been made redundant.' Unfortunately, however, there were still labour shortages and transportation problems. The pit closed in 1968.

The bridleway joins a road that leads to the school playing fields. Follow this, in front of the school buildings, to a wooden gate that leads to a public road. Turn right here and follow the road for about a mile. As is so often the case while walking in this rural area, it is very difficult to realise that just over thirty years ago a coal mine was operating here.

As you approach the crossroads you can see on your right the batch of New Rock and on the left the tree-covered batch of Old Rock colliery.

(Now the difficult route. From the junction of Abbey Road, Rock Road and the B3356, walk southwards along the B3356 until you reach the beginning of the industrial estate on your left. This is built on the site of New Rock Colliery. Before you come to the motor engineering building, there is a stile on the left. Cross the stile and keep to the right hand fence. This brings you to a kind of stile which takes you on to the lower part of the batch. This is not quite the route of the right of way on the map, but it seems to be well-used. Climb to the top of the batch from where you can look down on the site of New Rock Colliery. The one or two older brick-built buildings were probably the offices.

On the south side of the batch is a kind of gulley which leads down to the track of the incline. Follow this to the right until you come to a wire fence which is the boundary of the industrial estate. Turn left, forcing a way through the shrubbery if necessary. Cross the fence and walk south-westwards across the field to a stile and the playing fields of Downside School. Cross the field to the road. Now turn right along the road.)

At the crossroads turn left (signposted Shepton Mallet). This is the B3356 and soon you pass the entrance to what was once Old Rock Colliery, now Old Rock Farm.

Old Rock Colliery started in the 1780's and probably closed in the 1860's.

Behind Mendip View, a little further along the road, is a timber yard with a large building which was obviously one of the buildings of Strap Colliery.

Strap started in 1786 under the name of Downside Colliery. Then in 1862 the old shaft was deepened and the mine became known as Strap. By 1868 the company had run out of money as the mine went deeper and deeper. Work soon started again with new owners. Mining eventually started in 1869 and in 1874 the shaft was 1,838 feet deep, the deepest in Somerset. (Braysdown's shaft was 1,821 feet deep, but there was also a sump which took the mine an extra 30 feet!) It had been hoped that there would be a rail connection, but this never materialised and the pit closed in 1879. David Strawbridge comments that it must rank '... as one of the most expensive failures in Somerset's mining history.'

As has already been mentioned above, it was opened again for a short time in the 1960's, this time with the name Mendip Colliery.

Follow the road round to the left. There is a stile almost immediately on your right in the hedge. Cross the stile and note the derelict building on your left. This was part of Sweetleaze Colliery which lay between the road and the trees ahead.

By 1858 Sweetleaze had closed. It is uncertain when it first started work. However, a new winding engine was installed by 1862 and working resumed in the same year. It closed for the second and final time in 1879, the year that Strap closed.

Cross the field, bearing to the left towards the wooden stile which is in front of an older iron one, which is over a stone one. Cross, turn left and follow the path downhill through the woods to another stile and some stone steps. Here you come out of the woods. Turn right down hill and cross the old wooden stile or go through the gateway. There is a large iron pipe going down the valley side here, presumably connected to the old colliery. You are now in the Nettlebridge Valley walking upstream, though the path at first gradually descends the hillside.

At the next gateway there is a concrete water trough next to a hemispherical, metal one which looks vaguely industrial! After the next gateway I discovered a narrow stone tunnel in a kind of gulley down in the trees on the left. Perhaps it was once a drainage channel for one of the collieries.

Continue in the same direction. To the left is the wooded batch of Moorewood colliery, and behind the trees, the roof of one of the buildings is just visible. This was the winding house.

New Moorewood Colliery opened originally about 1870, but was flooded and closed in 1873. Westbury Iron Company was responsible for sinking the mine; it needed more coal to supplement what it already received from Newbury Colliery. (See Walk 12)

In 1913, the colliery reopened, the Beauchamp family having bought a major stake in it. A tramway was built up an incline and along the top of the valley to sidings next to the S & D. In about 1930 the tramway closed and road transport was used instead. The colliery closed in 1932 as there were problems with flooding and the coal being extracted was of poor quality.

The path now leads uphill. On the right, where the trees thin out, is what looks like a derelict limekiln. Follow the hedge on your left to the metal gate which leads to the road.

The old tramway ran under the road at this point and if you

look down to your left you can still see the entrance to the tunnel.
Turn right up the hill. At the top is a marvellous view of this
peaceful valley. Turn left along the road and where the road forks,
take the left-hand road - Coalpit Lane. The tramway was just the
other side of the hedge on the left. After 200 yards turn left down
the lane to Blackers Hill Farm. You can see some of the embankments
of the old fort on your left. Continue past the farm buildings, over
an old metal gate to the edge of the valley.

I have already referred to Robin Atthill's book and his chapter on
this valley. The lower part of this path has several names - Crock's
Bottom, Shawcross Bottom and the Romantic Valley. He talks of the
'utter quietness' of this stretch of the valley. As I walked down here
one December morning, the peace was shattered by the cracking of
shotguns at a pheasant shoot, with beaters calling and whistling,
and dogs barking. But soon the noise faded away as I walked on up
the valley, and I was alone in this valley, apart from one grazing
horse.

Turn right and follow the path down the side of the valley. At the
bottom, follow the path upstream, over the stile and through the
woods; then out into the open again. At the top of the field go through
the gate on the left into the lane. Turn right, but after a few yards,
turn left on up the valley. It is along here that you can see some
remains of buildings and old walls. Continue past the derelict
building on your left until you reach a metal gate in front of you.
Do not cross, but turn to the right, across the other metal gate.
Make your way up the hill to a wooden fence and go under the old
bridge which carried the tramway from Moorewood. To the left was
the tipping dock where coal was tipped from the tramway tubs into
standard-gauge wagons on the S & D. The railway went under the
road and on to Chilcompton. There is no longer a bridge here, but
the trackbed of the railway is still obvious.
Turn right and cross the metal gate on to Coalpit Lane. Turn
right along the road and notice on the left, behind a box hedge, the
shed which is constructed from an old railway carriage. Where the
road curves and dips down and meets the lane on your right, note

the bridge abutments of the old tramway. The road now rises out of the dip and just at the top there is a footpath sign on your left. Cross the metal gate and aim diagonally across the field to the gate which is to the left of the water trough. Carry on in the same direction, making towards the batch of New Rock Colliery in the distance. Where the hedge on the right ends, turn right and make for the two stiles and footbridge which are to the left of the farm buildings. Cross these and then cross another stile into the road. On the other side is a stile and the path heads towards the batch. In the corner of the field is a kissing gate. Follow the left-hand hedge to the road. Turn left to your starting point.

Above: Batch of New Rock Colliery.

11 Coleford, Edford and the Dorset and Somerset Canal

Distance: 3.5 miles
Starting point: King's Head, Coleford
Map Reference: 687487

This is a short walk, easy to follow, but with a high stile-quotient. There must be at least twenty – although some can be by-passed – and many of the instructions refer to 'another stile'. Practically all the paths are clearly signposted and one part that was particularly difficult to follow when I first walked here has been cleared up and greatly improved.

The very name Coleford suggests coal mining. At one time mining was a very important local occupation. Many of the early workings were shallow so that it is now impossible to say where they were with any certainty.

Starting from outside the King's Head in Coleford, set off eastwards along the road and cross what the Ordnance Survey now calls Mells Stream. Almost immediately on your right there is a metal stile which leads you to a track which follows the direction of the stream through woods. The track climbs uphill and then after another stile leads downhill to another stile by a stream. Cross this stile, go across the field to a gap in the hedge. There is a stile here on the left, but ignore this and turn right downhill to the gate. Go through the squeeze stile and cross back over the stream.

This is a packsaddle bridge and the OS map makes a point of noting this. Typically, a packsaddle bridge has a very low parapet, just a few inches high. A higher parapet might have interfered with the

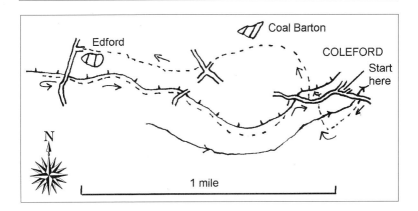

goods that were attached to either side of the pack-saddle. No doubt much traffic crossing this bridge in the distant past was on its way to the mill which is a few yards along the track. According to *The Batsford Guide to Industrial Archaeology of Central Southern England* by C.A. and R.A. Buchanan (Batsford, 1980) this mill, Sargent's Mill, was restored to working order and contains a breast shot wheel.

Follow the track, past the mill, to the road. Turn left, then after about 100 yards you come to the bottom of a steep hill. On the right is a lane which takes you up to the 'Hucky Duck' or aqueduct which crosses the lane.

In a pamphlet written about 1825, this aqueduct is described as 'noble and stupendous'. At one time there was a parapet which has since been removed for building stone, and this two-arched bridge may not seem quite so noble. However, when I first glimpsed it from the road on a cold, misty March day, it certainly surprised me. I had not expected anything quite so large in this small village. When I last walked here it was rather overgrown, but still impressive.

To the right of the gateway to the house, 'The Arches', which is on the other side of the 'Hucky Duck', there is a footpath which leads under the bridge and around the edge of the garden to a stile. Walk up the valley following the stream which is on the left. The track is quite well defined and probably led to the colliery of Coal Barton.

147

There is evidence of coal-tips along this track. On the right is a wood on a small hill and a stile on the left which is in line with the edge of the wood. The walk takes you across this stile, but, first, you might like to examine the ground under the trees. There is plenty of evidence of coal and waste. On the OS map a disused shaft is marked in the field up ahead.

This mine was Coal Barton pit. It is difficult to say how old it is, but in 1842 there were about 100 people working here. It finally closed in the 1850's.

Return to the stile which leads you across the stream, to another stile ahead and out into a field. The path leads diagonally towards the farm buildings. Between the red-tiled house and the farm is another stile which takes you on to a farm track and out to the road. Turn right up the road for a few yards. Cross the stile on the left and follow the right-hand hedge to another stile which brings you out on to a track to a house on your right. Almost straight ahead there is a well-defined path alongside the garden of the house. This curves round to yet another stile. Now bear slightly to the right across the field to a gap in the hedge. Follow the left-hand hedge to a gate and a stile (which seemed to have collapsed when I walked along here). Here you can see the premises of Stowell Concrete. This is the site of Edford Colliery.

Edford probably began working in the 1850's. There were coke ovens at the pit, and both coal and coke were being sent to Radstock to the railway in the 1880's. It closed in 1915 and now there are virtually no remains to be seen here.

Turn right, follow the track between the hedge and wire fence to the road that led to the colliery. Follow this to the T-junction.

In the fields on the other side of the road was the Blackpool Wood pit. This was started up by striking miners in 1921. However, it only lasted until 1923 when the drift broke into water.

Above: The Hucky-Duck (Aqueduct) at Coleford.

Below: Canal Bridge at Edford.

The road here can be quite busy with a large number of heavy lorries so take care. Turn left downhill. It is probably safer to walk on the left side of the road because of the bend further down.

On the bend, on the right side of the road, is a fence into a field. Cross into the field and walk to the small bridge which crosses the old Dorset and Somerset canal bed which you have just been walking along.

The canal carried on westwards for half a mile to its start where there was a rectangular basin. Work started here in 1796, and the canal had nearly reached Frome when the money ran out in 1803. To the west also lies Stratton Common or Stratton Moor, where pits were being worked as early as 1300. The coal outcrops at the surface, so that there were many workings which can still be discerned as small hillocks here and there. To the north there were very many shallow pits around the village of Holcombe. (It is well worth strolling around the village if you have time).

If you are interested in exploring this area there are several footpaths between Edford, Pitcot and Holcombe. There were larger pits at Barlake and Pitcot which closed in the second half of the 19th century.

Retrace your steps to the stile and the road. On the other side is another stile. Cross into the field. The walk now follows the route of the Dorset and Somerset Canal all the way back to Coleford and you can probably find your way without the need for instructions. The canal is on your left for most of the way and the path is quite obvious.

However, in case you get lost, here are detailed instructions!

The bed of the canal soon becomes clearly visible for a short distance, but the path leads into a wood, alongside the batch of Edford colliery on the left.

At one time this path was extremely difficult to follow because of the rubbish, blocks of stone and mud that had been deposited here, presumably when the colliery site was being tidied up for its new use. The path itself has now been tidied up, steps and wooden bridges have been installed and it is much easier to follow, although it can be slippery and muddy still.

Eventually you come to another stile and there again on the left is the canal bed. Follow it into the field and carry on in the same direction, cross a stile and then keep to the left-hand hedge. There is another stile and this leads you along the tow path, with the canal on your left and the garden of a house on your right. Now there is another stile. Keep closely to the right hand hedge. Another stile, to the road. This is the hamlet of Ham.

Ahead is another stile and you are back on the tow path. After several stiles through the woods, you come back into a field. After nearly 100 yards there is ... a stile on your left! This brings you back on to the tow path and there is quite a wide basin here. There is another stile in to a field and the track bed disappears, but carry on in the same direction close to the hedge on your left. Another stile appears at the end of the field on your left. Cross, turn right and head uphill to the gateway between a shed on the left and a wall on the right. Ahead is a gate. Go through on to the road and turn right downhill. This brings you back past the 'Hucky Duck', past the road to Sargents's Mill, and on to the King's Arms.

12 Coleford, Mells and Vobster

Distance:	5.5 miles
Starting point:	King's Head, Coleford
Map Reference:	687487

This walk begins by following the route of the Dorset and Somerset Canal to the collieries of Mackintosh and Newbury. From Newbury the canal was overlaid for part of its route by the Newbury Railway which was built by Westbury Iron Works from Mells Road station to serve the Newbury pit. The walk also passes Mells colliery before descending to the 'River without a name,' Robin Atthill's title for this stream in his *Old Mendip*. The OS has christened it Mells Stream.

The going is fairly easy, with a few stiles. Watch out for bulls though! One day I came across three on this route in different fields and, although they appeared to be friendly, I kept close to the hedge just in case I needed an escape route!

* *From the King's Head in Coleford go up the hill and follow the road round to the right as it ascends towards Highbury. Where the road flattens out for a few yards, just past the Wesleyan Methodist Chapel on the right, squeeze through the stile on the right and walk across the hillside towards the trees where you can see the bed of the D & S canal on your right. Looking ahead you can plainly see where it was built across the hillside. Cross a metal stile and another so that you are now on the right hand side of the canal. After another stile the ground flattens out and the canal is not obvious. Ahead, the path approaches another stile and woods. Turn left up the hill just before you reach the trees, following the hedge on your right. After*

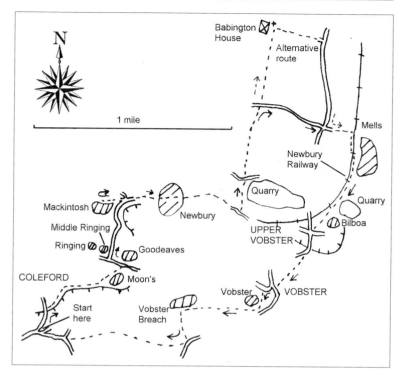

- a few yards there is a stile on your right. Cross it and make your
- way diagonally across the field, going uphill. Where the path joins
- a track you can see an overgrown dump which was the site of Moons
- colliery. The track leads you to the road.
- On the other side of the road is the site of the Goodeaves collieries.

At one time there were four shafts here, part of the Goodeaves
Colliery. It was working in 1824.

- Turn left along the road, then turn right along the road which is
- signposted Newbury, recycling centre and Natural Stone Products.

Where there is now a playing field on the left were once two pits,
New Ringing Pit and Middle Ringing Pit. They were abandoned
about 1830.

At the bottom of the hill the road follows the bend of the Dorset and Somerset Canal which then curved round in front of the miners' cottages. It was intended that the canal would go through a tunnel from the other side of the hill. On the left you can see the batch of Mackintosh Colliery. At the small crossroads there is a track to the left up to the site of Mackintosh Colliery. There is not a great deal to be seen, though, on the other side of the stile, you can see the remains of a brick building which has some metal 'thing' embedded into the wall and beyond you can see a concrete platform which is presumably the top of the shaft. Looking back down the track you can see the site of Newbury Colliery, now belonging to Natural Stone Products. The track is where the incline ran, joining the two collieries.

Originally there were, according to Down and Warrington, a host of small pits around the small hamlet of Newbury, a short distance to the north. One, Old Newbury Colliery was sunk about 1710, but this one took over and was working at the beginning of the 19th century. When Westbury Iron Works opened in 1857, much of the coal and coke was sent there and eventually the Iron Works took control. Mackintosh Colliery opened in 1867 as part of the same business concern. For a time Mackintosh, and perhaps Newbury, closed because of lack of trade at the end of the century. In 1919 Mackintosh was flooded and had to close permanently. Newbury closed in 1927 after financial troubles. Down and Warrington's 'The Newbury Railway' has some fascinating photographs of both these pits and Mells Collieries, as well as some detailed diagrams and plans.

Make your way into the site of Newbury Colliery, taking care because of the sometimes heavy traffic, and follow the footpath signs that have very sensibly been erected by the company. You need to follow the blue arrows. In the yard you can see the building that once housed the Cornish beam engine which was used to pump water out of the pit.

Bear to the right then make your way down the ramp into the lower yard. To your left was a line of coke ovens. Walk diagonally

> *across the yard and at the end of the large shed, turn right towards*
> *the end of the site. (If you are not sure of the direction, head towards*
> *the power line posts). Between the blocks of stone you will find a*
> *final arrow which leads you on to the track bed of the railway and*
> *canal. Follow the left hand hedges until you reach the houses of*
> *Upper Vobster. There is a stile on your left here which leads on to a*
> *narrow road. After 50 yards there is a lane between the houses on*
> *your left leading to a stile.*
>
> *Before taking this path, you may wish to walk the short distance*
> *to where, on your left, were the sidings of Vobster quarry.*

When Westbury Iron works opened, it also needed limestone for its blast furnaces and Vobster quarry was able to provide it. The ironworks leased the quarry and constructed a limekiln. A narrow gauge railway ran through a tunnel from the sidings into the quarry itself.

> *Return to the path between the houses, cross the stile and head north,*
> *following the high wire fence on your right. Occasionally, there are*
> *glimpses of the water-filled lake through the trees.*
>
> *Cross the stile into the road and turn right for a few yards to the*
> *stile on your left. Cross into the field, follow the right hand hedge,*
> *go through another gateway and head for the gateway to the left of*
> *the aptly named White Cottage.*

On the opposite side of the road are two impressive gateposts, though no gate. The path between the, mainly, beech trees leads to Babbington House, now a country club. Further on you might be able to glimpse Ammerdown House in amongst the trees and to the right the column on the Ammerdown estate. This was designed by Joseph Jopling in the form of Eddystone Lighthouse, with a glass dome on top (though this was missing the last time I walked here) in 1853. You can also see Cley hill to the east and Downside Abbey to the west.

The house, with its seven-bay facade, was built about 1700 by Henry Mompesson and there is a tiny church in front of Babbington House, built in 1750. It is well worth looking at so if you fancy a

Left: Mells Colliery Engine House.

Below: Canal Bridge, Upper Vobster.

156

slightly longer walk you could walk along the path ahead to the house, turn right along the drive to the road, turn right again along the busy road to rejoin the route to Mells Colliery.

If you are not taking the detour, turn right along the road and, when you reach the main road, cross straight over into the lane that led to Mells Colliery. As you approach the site there is a stile on your right. There are still some red brick buildings, including the engine house which can be seen a little further along the path.

Mells Colliery opened in the 1860's. It worked for 20 years then closed. It was reopened in 1909, but working conditions were very poor and, as usual, there were financial difficulties. This situation lasted throughout the 20's and 30's, the real losers being the miners who had to accept low wages and eventually the sack. Despite changes in ownership, the pit remained unprofitable and closed in 1943.

Cross the stile and walk alongside the route of the railway (and of the canal) on your left. After 80-90 yards there is another stile which takes you into the site of the colliery. You can now see the old engine house. The new buildings seem to have been constructed around the supports of the colliery screens. Above them was the shaft and pithead.

Straight ahead is another stile. Drop down to the field and follow the left-hand hedge and the low railway embankment. Continue following the left-hand hedge. It becomes a fence and then curves round to the right to a gate and a stile. You have been following the route of the railway. From here it curved towards the road on your right and as you cross the next field you should be able to see the bridge under the road.

On your left is the site of Bilboa quarry, now flooded! This quarry had its own railway connection for a while stemming from the GWR a short distance east of Mells Road station where the Newbury Railway started. This quarry closed about 1933. There was another colliery here, close to the road you are approaching, also called Bilboa. It was older than Mells and little is known about it.

The footpath goes diagonally across the field to the crossroads known as Vobster Cross. Head for the group of trees in which are several tall conifers.

There is a sign on the stile warning you to take care here. The road can be very busy and much of the traffic turns quickly in front of you on the way to Mells village and the surrounding quarries.

Take the road to the south, signposted Lower Vobster etc. After 100 yards the road crosses the route of the canal, where there are some metal railings on the right. If you lean over you can see the outline of the arch. You can also see clearly the route.

A few yards down the hill, cross the stile on your left, and bear to the right across the field towards the hedge. On your left is the embankment of the incline of the railway which led to Vobster and Vobster Breach collieries. Ahead you can see Melcombe Wood.

There were many pits along the far side of the valley where the coal outcropped. Down and Warrington estimate that there were at least 50 pits to the south and south-east of Vobster and probably as many again of which the sites are unknown.

There is a stile in the hedge, some yards to the right of the incline. Walk straight ahead and then descend to the Vobster Inn, a welcome sight at this stage of the walk!

Turn right to the T-junction, then turn left along the Coleford road. Just past the last cottage on the left there is a gate and a stile into a field. Although the footpath sign seems to be pointing up the hill, follow the left-hand hedge to another stile, cross the stream and another stile into a field. Now cross the field, following the just recognisable stone track, cross the ditch, carry on for a few yards uphill, and then turn right through the middle of a small spoil heap. On the left are the remains of some stone buildings. On the right is more evidence of Vobster Colliery.

It is not known when Vobster Colliery opened. There were three shafts and, although the winding gear was operated by a steam engine, water was pumped out by using water wheels. It probably closed about 1875. There was a tramway which led to Bilboa Colliery at Vobster Cross and which also extended westwards to Vobster Breach Colliery.

- *Cross another stile and follow the raised track of the old tramway. Go through the next gateway, and bear slightly to the right towards the trees. You should be able to see a stile in the hedge. Notice that the trees ahead seem to be in rows. They follow the line of the old coke ovens. Cross the stiles and turn immediately left. Cross one line of ovens and then turn right. Walk between the trees and the remains of the ovens. Some of them still have their arches standing. This is the site of Vobster Breach Colliery.*

Vobster Breach was sunk to connect with a seam which was being worked at Vobster. In 1861 the connection was made and two rows of coke ovens were built. It closed at about the same time as Vobster.

It was in these pits and in others in the area that the seams were often vertical so that coal had to be extracted in a different manner to other seams. Miners would work the seam above their heads, supporting themselves on beams of wood, gradually replacing the beams at a higher level.

- *You are now standing between the two lines of coke ovens which once had tramway sidings between them. At the end, where you come out into the open, you can see on your right the batch and ahead the wall of what might have been the building where the winding shaft was situated. Turn left now and head towards an old gateway. Here were the offices. Make your way to the metal gate, then turn right towards the oak tree. Further on there is a gap between the hedge on your right. Cross the field, keeping to the left-hand hedge.*

On the opposite side of the valley, to the north, is Stock Hill where at one time there were many small pits.

- *The path continues westwards, across three fields. It becomes a stone track and brings you to the Coleford-Leigh upon Mendip road. Turn right down the hill towards the starting point at the King's Head.*

More books on Somerset from Ex Libris Press:

GEOLOGY OF SOMERSET
by Peter Hardy
224 pages; Fully illustrated; ISBN 0 948578 42 4; Price £9.95

CHEDDAR VALLEY RAILWAY WALK
by Douglas Kidder
128 pages; Fully illustrated; ISBN 0 948578 44 0; Price £5.95

WEST MENDIP WAY
by Derek Moyes
96 pages, Fully illustrated; ISBN 0 948578 45 9; Price £4.95

WHERE WILTSHIRE MEETS SOMERSET
20 Best Walks around Bath, Bradford on Avon,
Trowbridge, Westbury, Warminster and Frome
by Roger Jones
128 pages; Illustrated throughout; ISBN 0 948578 94 7; Price £5.95

THE MENDIPS
by Robin & Romy Williams
176 pages; Illustrated throughout; ISBN 0 948578 76 9; Price £7.95

THE SOMERSET LEVELS
by Robin & Romy Williams
176 pages; Illustrated throughout; ISBN 0 948578 38 6; Price £7.95

WELLS: AN HISTORICAL GUIDE
by Martin Langley
104 pages; Illustrated throughout; ISBN 0 948578 24 6; Price £5.95

Books from Ex Libris Press are obtainable through your local
bookshop or direct from the publisher post-free on receipt of net
price, as above.
Ask for a free copy of our illustrated complete list of books.

EX LIBRIS PRESS
1 The Shambles, Bradford on Avon, Wiltshire, BA15 1JS
Tel/Fax 01225 863595
e mail: roger@ex-libris.jpcinet.co.uk